# The
# Single
# African-American
# Christian

# The Single African-American Christian

MAINTAINING A CLEAN LIFE IN A DIRTY WORLD

Eddie B. Lane

First published in 1993 as
*Maximizing Your Singleness: Going for the Gold*
Copyright © 1993, 1994

All rights reserved.

Publisher:
Black Family Press
1810 Park Row
Dallas, Texas 75215
(214) 428-3761

Published in the United States of America

Cover design: Fame Publishing Inc.

Black Family Press
Copyright ©1995 Eddie B. Lane

# TABLE OF CONTENTS

# ACKNOWLEDGMENTS

This book is dedicated to my four children, Kenneth, Felicia, Carla, and Eddie whom I love dearly. My children have been for me—and their mother—a laboratory of experiences and testing that have given rise to the confirmation of the faithfulness of God in the area of growing children into healthy adults.

As teenagers and as adults, my children have demonstrated that God's standards of morality are possible through His power. They have also proven that adherence to the Christian standard of moral purity enhances one's chance of accomplishing personal and professional goals.

My children are not perfect; they all have their failures. By the grace of God, however, they have demonstrated a love for Jesus Christ and His church.

I must also acknowledge many friends who have helped me think and rethink my ideas about single life. Some worked with the organization and layout; some edited and typed the manuscripts; while others provided immeasurable resources. Although the list is much too long to mention, some must be noted. They are: Lafayette E. Holland, Mary A. Wallace, Jannica Green, Stephen E. Slocum Jr., Don and Charlotte Test, Lin Williams, Mary H. Crossland, and Billie Stafford.

I am deeply indebted to Bibleway Bible Church and all the members who have supported me in various ways over the years . . . giving me the liberty to grow and develop a number of ministries within and outside the church.

# FOREWORD

In the many years in which I have served as a pastor of a local church in Dallas, Texas, I have observed that the single life for African-Americans is both challenging and rewarding. It is challenging in that there is an imbalance in the ratio of available males to females and rewarding in the freedom it affords one to explore life with Jesus Christ . . . unencumbered, fully involved in Christian service.

The focus here is on the choices and challenges of living the Christian life as a single Christian in the social context of a society that has lost its sense of moral purity.

It is my conviction that these are days in which the difference between a continued deterioration of the family and the cycle of violence in the African-American community is the difference between the presence of moral convictions or the absence of such convictions. Thus, I seek to make a case for a Christian lifestyle for single African-American men and women, who are Christians.

The decision to emphasize the African or Black American Christian is an attempt to note that there are significant differences between the context of these Christians and singles of other races. These differences are not in what the Bible teaches about morality—for what the Bible says to one race, it says to all races. The differences lie in the spiritual, social, economic, and domestic context in which the African-American lives.

This author writes to the African-American single against the background of slavery, segregation, economic deprivation, and political disenfranchisement. The distinctive role of the Black church in this history as well as the persistent reality of racial prejudice and discrimination today are crucial considerations.

It is only the African-American race whose women outnumber their men on an average of five to one. It is the African-American race whose women on average earn more annually than do the men, and it is only the African-American race whose men fill the prisons of America on an average of 40 to 60 percent. It is the African-American who must look exclusively to the local church for help in managing life as a single Christian. Thus I have sought to make a case for the single African-American Christian.

# CHAPTER 1

# THE CHRISTIAN ATTITUDE TOWARDS SEX

Today it is not uncommon to find the single Christian and the single nonChristian sharing a common lifestyle in almost every area of life, including their sexual behavior. Indeed, some have come to believe that there is really no distinction that can be made between the Christian single and the nonChristian single in terms of general attitude and behavior in the area of sex and sexuality. Thus, as it pertains to sexual attitudes and sexual behavior, it is felt that there are no specific practical and attitudinal differences. This assumed common ground in the areas of sexual attitude and behavior between the Christian and the nonChristian must, at the least, be viewed as an optical illusion for there are vast differences between the Christian and the nonChristian from a biblical perspective. The basic difference is that the Christian and the nonChristian belong to two very different masters who share no common ground—moral or spiritual (2 Cor. 6:14ff.). Moreover, saved singles have been born again with a new heart and a new life that calls for a new way of thinking and acting in every area of their lives, including their morality.

In 1 Thessalonians, the Lord reminded the Church, including the singles, how they had come to a saving knowledge of Jesus Christ through the preaching of the gospel. They had experienced the saving power of the gospel which they believed and it had changed their lives, and the change was to be evident in their behavior. However, in the church at Thessalonica, there were new Christians who were not sure about how they should behave as it related to their sexual standards and other matters. The church of that day seemed to have been uncertain as to whether to denounce or affirm sex outside the bounds of marriage. Sexual freedom and the pursuit of pleasure were the common attitude and practice of that day, as it is in our day; therefore, the Church itself was uncertain.

## Two Essentials

This uncertainty on the part of the new believers at Thessalonica as to how they were to behave morally now that they were saved reflected two significant deficits in their newly developing Christian world view. First, as new believers there was a deficiency in their *knowledge* of the word of God. Second, there was a deficit in the number of models within the local church based on Scripture.

The problem was not that these believers were without divine revelation concerning the moral behavior of Christians. These new believers needed to be taught what the Word of God said in this area. In time, the number of models of Christian morality would be increased as these new believers matured in the faith.

## The Importance of Discipling

In our day there is a similar deficit in the knowledge of the Word of God in the minds and hearts of believers, both married and single, regarding what the Bible says regarding moral behavior. This lack of knowledge is not due to the silence of the text on the subject of Christian morality, but the absence of effective *discipleship*, especially of single African-American adult males in our churches.

Like the church at Thessalonica, there are in the African-American community too few models of single adults whose morality is motivated by biblically-based convictions. I have found that the single adults in our churches are most often neither visible or vocal about their singleness. This is because there is a sense in which people imply by their attitude and sometimes even by what they say that there is something unnatural in being single and abstaining from sex.

I, like many African-American males, grew up in a cultural context in which it was expected as a sign of your genuine manliness to have sex with as many girls as you possibly could. In this kind of environment, virginity for a boy was frowned upon even by church-going parents. As a young man growing up and attending church on a regular basis, I never heard a sermon on morality. Unfortunately, in today's pulpits, in all too many instances the message has not changed.

The lack of biblical knowledge, combined with a shortage of visible models and silence in the pulpits on the subject of morality, often gives new believers in our churches a sense of liberty in their moral attitudes and behavior. Their sexual behavior is more consistent with their old life as an unbeliever than it is with their new life in Christ. In other words, some new believers have a sense of liberty in their morality that the Bible does not grant them. Therefore, there is a serious need for the single Christian, both male and female, to be discipled by more mature, preferably single Christians, resulting in their understanding what the Bible says regarding moral behavior, and subsequently their becoming visible and vocal models of that truth themselves.

## MAXIMIZING YOUR SINGLENESS

In 1 Thessalonians 4, the Lord responds to this unsettled question in the minds of the Thessalonian believers by giving them absolute instruction about how they were to live now that they were new creations in Christ (2 Cor. 5:17). Regarding their sex life the text says, "This is the will of God for you, your sanctification" (1 Thess. 4:3). As it pertains to maximizing one's singleness, the first order of business is choosing to live a life that has as its distinction the mark of *spiritual sanctification*. For unless or until the Christian, whether single or married, is willing to live a sanctified lifestyle, there is no need of even thinking of going for the goal of a qualitative, abundant life in Christ (John 10:10).

## THE MEANING OF SANCTIFICATION

At the very start it is important that we understand that sanctification has three phases: positional sanctification, progressive sanctification and ultimate sanctification. Positional sanctification is the believer's *spiritual position* in Christ received at the moment of salvation. Progressive sanctification is the believer's *choice of lifestyle* in which he/she abstains from sin in view of a new position in Christ. Finally ultimate sanctification is the believer's *deliverance from the very presence of sin at death* when he/she enters into the presence of the Lord in heaven.

In maximizing one's singleness through a sanctified life, it is imperative that the single person understands that a primary difference exists between the single saved person and the single unsaved person. The single saved person has a spiritual position in Christ Jesus. This means the saved single has been set apart unto God and apart from the devil. Secondly, saved singles are called to a sanctified lifestyle. Among other things, this means that saved singles understand that it is the will of God for them to choose to abstain from sexual sin. This challenge of the single's sexual choices focuses on the saved single's experiential walk with God in cooperation with the Holy Spirit. In sharp contrast, the unsaved single has no such understanding about the will of God. This does not mean that unsaved singles are necessarily immoral. It does mean, however, that their moral convictions are not based on a conviction about the will of the living God for their lives.

## LIVING A SANCTIFIED LIFE

In the area of progressive sanctification, the Christian's role is one of cooperation with the Holy Spirit.

This is not a "let go and let God experience." Instead, the Bible is very specific when it says:

"Having therefore these promises, dearly beloved, let us cleanse ourselves from all filthiness of the flesh and spirit, perfecting holiness in the fear of God" (2 Cor. 7:1).

"Flee from idolatry" (1 Cor. 10:14).

"Flee also youthful lust, but follow righteousness, faith, charity, peace, with them that call on the Lord out of a pure heart" (2 Tim. 2:22).

"Meditate upon these things; give thyself wholly to them; that thy profiting may appear to all" (1 Tim 4:15).

From these and many other passages, it is clear that, as it pertains to progressive sanctification, believers have a primary responsibility that requires action on their part. One major area of that responsibility is to choose to cooperate with the Holy Spirit in the choice of lifestyle. The believer who is living a sanctified life is one who has a spiritual agenda and is willing to sacrifice. It is not possible for the secular minded Christian to live a sanctified lifestyle.

## THE KEY IS DEDICATION

It is important that it be understood that if you are saved but have not dedicated your life to Jesus Christ (Rom. 12:1-2), this is a step you must take right now. Christians who are not dedicated to Jesus Christ can not maximize their singleness through victorious living in this area of moral choices. If you are not dedicated to Jesus Christ, a sanctified lifestyle is far beyond your spiritual reach. Once again, you need to be reminded that the Bible says: "For this is the will of God for you, your sanctification" (1 Thess. 4:3). This is clearly stated and is an inescapable truth for you and for me as believers.

As a Christian, commitment to lead a sanctified life is a vital first step to all that follows. The most frustrated believers I know and have ever ministered to are those who try to live up to God's standard of morality without being committed to the Lord in every area of life. Liz was just such a person. She came to Christ and abandoned her old relationships, vowing to live a moral life for Jesus. This radical change in her behavior was not accompanied by involvement in a strong discipleship program. Thus, the change created a serious void in her life. Within a few months, Liz found herself back in her old ways, because while trying to keep her moral commitment, she disregarded her spiritual responsibilities in other areas of her life. Sanctification demands the wholeness of the believer—body, mind, and spirit (Rom. 6:12ff.).

## THE POWER SOURCE FOR VICTORIOUS SINGLE LIVING

While riding down Martin Luther King Boulevard in South Dallas on the way to my office, I began to pay particular attention to the number of liquor trucks that frequent the community stocking and restocking the many liquor stores with various kinds of alcoholic beverages. There was no chance of any establishment experiencing a shortage with this constant replenishing.

It occurred to me that the people who are the customers of these liquor stores find in the content of the liquor something that stimulates their spirit in such a way that it causes them to feel and experience some things that they could not otherwise feel and experience. It was evident that they liked the experience.

I have thought further about the evident human need for the incorporation of another spirit into one's body. Indeed a spirit that could cause the individual to feel and act in a way that is not common to his/her natural behavior. Based on the number of people who drink liquor, I concluded that there must be in most folk a need to feel and experience a kind of spirit and energy that moves them beyond themselves. In this context of thinking about the evident general human need for some kind of liquid spirit to stimulate the human spirit, my mind moved from the liquor stores and their stock of liquid spirits to the church house and our emphasis on the Holy Spirit. There is a parallel between what the person gets from the liquor store, namely, liquor and drugs (spirits) of one kind or the other and what a person gets from the church, namely, the Holy Spirit of God. They are alike in that they both stimulate the inner spirit of the person who ingests them.

I think that people who drink liquor and take drugs to the point that they are controlled by them do so for various reasons. Some see it as an avenue of escape; others need a stimulus to "face up" to something. Many want to feel a certain way, behave differently or verbalize something. Their natural spirit inhibits them. They need something more than what is naturally possessed to get them where they feel they need or want to be.

So it is with Christians. There is a need in our lives for a spirit energizer that moves us out and beyond our natural spirit into an area of feeling and acting that is foreign to our natural selves. For the Christian that spirit is none other than the Holy Spirit of God. Ephesians 5:18 focuses on the need for human spirit stimulation in the lives of Christians. It offers an alternative to alcoholic beverages and drugs as that spirit energizer. "Be not drunk with wine wherein there is excess" (Eph. 5:18). The text is saying that for the Christian drunkenness is unacceptable. Note the fact that there is implied in this statement that even Christians need their spirits stimulated. However, the option for the Christian is not spirit stimulation by wine but rather, spirit stimulation by way of the Holy Spirit.

In terms of spirit stimulation: the church is to the child of God what the liquor stores and drug dealers are to the indulging person. Both are sources from which one finds that which stimulates the spirit. The believer can no more stay away from the church in search of that spiritual stimulus than the drunkard can stay away from the liquor store in search of alcoholic stimulus.

The emphasis here is on drunkenness not drinking. Again the issue is not "to drink or not to drink," but drunkenness. The means by which the Christian can become drunk and thus controlled by it is either alcohol or the Holy Spirit. Both will produce the same effect: actions contrary to one's natural self.

On the Day of Pentecost the Holy Spirit came and filled the Apostles. Peter and the others began to preach Christ crucified and resurrected in the language of all the people who were present. Those who knew them thought they were drunk. Peter responded to this by saying that it was too early in the morning for them to be drunk. They concluded that Peter was filled with the Holy Spirit of God. So when I say to you that there is similarity between the behavior of a person who is drunk on alcohol and the person who is filled with the Spirit, I am in good company. The difference is in the cause of the behavior and the nature of the behavior.

Attached to drunkenness is the phrase "wherein there is excess." Not only does alcohol cause the person to act in ways contrary to their natural behavior, but the nature of the behavior is characterized by excess or debauchery. To understand the concept of excess or debauchery in Ephesians 5:18, one may look at the prodigal son who wasted both his life and his money (Luke 15:11-32). He lived a life of excess. On the other hand, Acts 2 is an example of what behavior is like when one is filled with the Spirit. It is a life of extraordinary behavior . . . controlled, in order, no excesses.

The command for the Christian is to be drunk on the Holy Spirit. To be filled with the Holy Spirit is to be controlled by the Holy Spirit in the same way that excessive wine controls the one who drinks it. Some think that being filled with the Holy Spirit is about being saved. These people also think that the evidence of a Spirit filled life is found in the ability to speak in tongues. Such is not the case. The filling of the Spirit is about energizing the human spirit so that the believer is able to feel, think, and act in ways that are contrary to his/her natural human spirit.

The beer commercials on television are filled with images that set before us the notion that this or that kind of beer will enable young men and women to feel and act in ways that are more than a little bit exciting. It could well be said that a day on the beach is not what it could be without a trunk full of cold beer. Football and other sports are not as exciting to watch without liquor. Sex is not as intense without the enhancement of potent beer. Thus, the alcoholic beverage industry has reached a multimillion dollar level.

Let me carefully make the comparison that the church needs to emulate the liquor industry and advocate that life is not all that it can be without the enabling influence of the Holy Spirit on our human spirit. "Be not drunk with wine but be filled with the Holy Spirit," the text says.

The Spirit-filled life is not easily concealed. It will show up in how the believer behaves in public and in private. The Spirit-filled life has two significant effects on the believer. First, it enables believers to live life wisely rather than unwisely. Second, it enables believers to have and maintain a life of praise and worship of the living God. Three signs of a Spirit-filled life are found in Scripture. Ephesians 5:19-20 says, "Speaking to one another in psalms and hymns and spiritual songs singing and making melody with your heart to the Lord; always giving thanks for all things in the name of our Lord Jesus Christ to God, even the Father; and be subject to one another in the fear of Christ."

First, we must note that being filled with the Spirit is a command from God to every believer. It is the believer's choice to obey or disobey this command. But for every believer who elects to be filled with the Spirit of God there is the experience of not being depressed or down in his/her spirit. The Spirit-filled child of God is one who is "up" on the inside. The Spirit of God, when controlling the human spirit of the believer, elevates the mind of the believer above circumstances. In spite of any current adverse situation one might be in, he/she is able to encourage others and sing praises to the living Lord. When the Spirit of God is controlling your life you will have a melody of praise in your heart to the Lord and you will be a source of encouragement to others.

The command to be filled with the Spirit is in the present passive tense. This means that in terms of being filled with the Spirit, no effort is necessary on the part of the believer. Rather, the believer must yield his/her mind to the power and influence of the Holy Spirit.

The "singing and making melody in your heart to the Lord" is not the way the believer rises to the point of being filled with the Spirit. No, this singing and making melody in the heart is the result of believers being filled with the Spirit.

The second sign of a Spirit-controlled life is an attitude of thankfulness to God for all the various circumstances that one experiences from day to day. The Spirit of God enables Christians to trust God to always do what is best for them. The Spirit of God causes believers to believe that whatever it is that God allows to come into their life is for their good no matter how it appears at that moment. Thus, there is the consistent attitude of thankfulness.

Third, the Spirit-filled life is a life characterized by a spirit of submissiveness. Stubbornness is not the way of life for the Spirit-filled believer. I take it that the Spirit-filled child of God is one who yields his/her will to the will of another believer.

## CONCLUSION

The filling of the Spirit is tied to the challenge of both living the Christian life and doing effective ministry in the context of an evil and perverted generation of people. To the extent that we the church recognize the impossibility of our meeting the challenge of living and serving the Lord effectively and consistently . . . to that extent we will yield ourselves to the power of the Holy Spirit within us.

The filling of the Spirit is a matter of obedience to the Lord's command. It is not something that we must seek to try to rise to with religious activity. To be filled with the Spirit is to obey God's command and yield to the Spirit.

In Acts 1 we have the record of the Lord Jesus standing on a mountain just outside of the Jerusalem bidding farewell to His disciples. In Acts 1:8 Jesus specifically instructs His disciples not to leave the city nor to attempt to carry on the mission that He had begun with them until the Holy Spirit came and indwelled them thus empowering them for ministry. "You shall receive power," Jesus said to His disciples, "when the Holy Spirit has come upon you; and you shall be My witnesses both in Jerusalem and in all Judea and Samaria, and even to the remotest part of the earth."

In Acts 2 the Spirit came and empowered the disciples. They lost their fear of the crowd who had crucified Jesus and they went out and began to preach in and around Jerusalem and then in Judea.

The filling of the Holy Spirit is about the power to serve the Lord, not about making noise in church on Sunday. Spirit-filled Christians are Christians on a mission for Jesus Christ and that mission is winning the lost to Christ through preaching Christ. It is not a mission of Sunday morning hand-waving.

After the Spirit came, Peter and John met a lame man in the vicinity of the temple. The man asked Peter and John for money. Peter answered, "I do not possess silver and gold, but what I do have I give to you: In the name of Jesus Christ the Nazarene—walk!" (Acts 3:6). The filling of the Spirit is about serving power. Thus, when the church sings songs of joy and praise there is power in the singing. When the church prays there is power in the prayer.

There may be failures in your life that you are not pleased with. It may be that you have found that the more you have learned about the Lord in His word, the more difficult it has become for you to do what you know to do. You need the filling of God's Spirit in your life. For when the Spirit is in control, you can live skillfully doing that which is pleasing to the Lord.

# CHAPTER 2

# PURITY AND CHRISTIAN COMMITMENT

Sex can be a troubling problem for many single people even though they are Christians. Although it is not a problem that is unique to the single person, all too often it is a problem that a single person who is walking with God must reckon with. As Christians it is time that we face up to the fact that it can be a very real struggle.

## THREE EXAMPLES

I am reminded of a young single man that I pastored; I will call him Bill. In his early thirties, he had recently been saved from a life of gross immorality. Now that Bill was saved he was obviously struggling with his sexual desires. His struggle became evident to the congregation in short order. Every time the church gathered for prayer, this young single man would jump to his feet and ask for prayer for control in his sex life. He wanted us to pray that God would keep him morally pure. It wasn't long before everyone in the congregation looked at Bill in anticipation of his persistent request for this critical struggle in this area of his life. It was obvious to all of us that Bill did not have the gift of self control so that for him abstaining from sex now that he was saved was a serious matter. In God's providence, the church's prayers were answered: God gave Bill a wife.

Another case comes to mind in this area of facing the reality of sexual struggle as a saved single. Keith, unlike Bill, refused to acknowledge the reality of his struggle in abstaining from sexual immorality. To even acknowledge the presence of sexual desires, much less the reality of his struggle, was tantamount to admitting to being in sin. Ultimately, Keith's failure to face up to his struggle lead to repeated failure in this area of his life.

A third case is Charles, who for the sake of the ministry, not only chose to remain single, but also to remain morally pure. This young man while acknowledging the presence of his sexual desires, found the strength to not fulfill these desires. The difference in this young adult was not just the decision to be a moral person, but that this young single adult, unlike the other two, found that his call to serve God came with the gift of self-control. There was an important second difference between Charles and the other two men: Charles was a virgin at age thirty-five.

## BIOLOGY VERSES SPIRITUAL COMMITMENT

The issue is not a matter of biology in terms of the degree of sexual urges and peer pressure experienced by the saved and unsaved single adult. The difference is a difference of spiritual commitment and spiritual conviction. The libido of the saved person is no different from the libido or sex drive of the unsaved person. The difference in their moral behavior, however, can be attributed to their relationship or lack of relationship with God and their commitment to His way. I often hear single men who do not abstain declare that their sexual appetites are greater than those singles who somehow are able to abstain from sex. My response is that the issue of morality is not a matter of sexual intensity or the degree of pressure experienced. Abstinence for the Christian is a matter between the single person, his body which is the temple of God, and his God whose temple he is. Morality is not just a matter of human resolve, but a matter of obedience to and dependence upon the living God.

It should be kept in mind that the problem that sex presents to the single person who knows the Lord as Savior is not only a spiritual *challenge* that demands a response, but also an exciting *opportunity* to be faithful to God's Holy Word in spite of the pressure of the society around us. Faithfulness in this important area will not only give honor to the Lord but will give one great personal joy.

My home town of Lake Providence, Louisiana made the news in *Time Magazine*, August 15, 1994, as the poorest town in America. As I read that article I was reminded that a primary contributing factor to my not being trapped in that poor city was my commitment early in my life to moral purity. This commitment lead me to marriage at age twenty-one. All of my children have been born to the same woman and in my own nest. *There is great profit in moral purity.*

I am reminded of the passage that says that godliness with contentment is great gain (1 Tim. 6:6). Profit in moral purity is evident in the number of young men and women who achieve academic excellence in high school and subsequently receive scholarships. When they arrive on the college campus they discover that there is an absence of structured external moral restraints to govern their moral behavior similar to what they had at home. This new freedom lends itself to open assault on the moral convictions of these young people and the moral challenge proves to be a much greater challenge than the college curriculum. Their failure to make the cut morally costs them their college career and spoils their potential for success in their chosen professions. *There is great benefit in moral purity.*

As my daughters entered college, I told them, "Make sure your natural biological desires are not allowed to hold your brain hostage." What I wanted them to do was to discipline their minds so they were in control of their biological drives rather than their biological drives being in control of their college careers.

I am always amazed at the number of females who, because of the lack of commitment to moral purity, get pregnant and drop out of school. I am equally astonished by the number of males whose careers are stymied by sexual immorality. It is my contention that moral purity is not only the righteous way to live before God as a Christian, but it is also a profitable lifestyle in terms of developing holistically and obtaining professional goals. *Moral purity is of great practical value.*

## THE BIBLICAL ABSOLUTE

If you, as a Christian young person, are looking for the Bible's teaching as it pertains to sex for the single person, the word from God is *abstain.* This principle of abstention from sex as a single person is not a relative principle that is to be applied depending on circumstances. It is unconditional . . . imperative.

Since abstaining from sex as a single person is an absolute, it is an issue that must be faced. The application of this principle requires discipline which is the fruit of spiritual commitment. You see, it does not require any discipline to abstain from that which one does not desire. Neither does it require discipline to abstain from that which one wants but cannot get. To abstain from that which one wants and can have, but must not, requires the kind of discipline that can only come as the fruit of spiritual commitment.

If we are to believe the media, the entertainment industry and even some religious organizations, we are to conclude that morality is relative. There are no absolutes in morality. This kind of thinking is in direct opposition to what the Bible teaches. For the Christian, morality is tied to biblical absolutes.

## AN ALARMING SHORTAGE

In the African-American community today, single women outnumber single men on the order of five to one. This serious shortage of African-American men is caused by a number of factors: 40 to 60 percent of them are locked up in jails, state and federal prisons; vast numbers are killed in black-on-black crime; the mortality rate for infant males is high; and an inordinate number of casualties occurred during military conflicts and wars (killed and disabled). These are just a few of the reasons why there is such a shortage of marriageable African-American men. Then there are the victims of AIDS, homicide, and homosexuality. Let us not forget those men who exclusively choose to date and marry women of other ethnicities. This means that many African-American single women may not have the choice of marrying an African-American. Even the choice of someone to date is a limited possibility for four out of every five women.

The contrast is even more troubling in the African-American church where women outnumber the men on the average of eight to one. For the African-American female, marriage is not something that can be taken for granted. Indeed, the normal stages of dating, courting, engagement, marriage, and children all too often never happens. Few can imagine the frustration of waiting seemingly in vain. This is truly a sad commentary on our times.

In addition, if you are a Christian, you must face the issue of being unequally yoked together with an unbeliever (2 Cor. 6:14). Of all the horror stories I have in my memory bank of people I have pastored, none are as severe and heartbreaking as those of saved men and women who chose to disregard this prohibition from the Lord and have proceeded to marry an unbeliever. In all my many years in the pastorate, I have yet to see a single case in which the Christian who married an unsaved person ended up winning that person to Christ. It may happen, but it has not in my experience.

Over the years, I have observed that a woman who has had a relationship with a man, and for whatever reason finds herself without a male companion, will experience a sense of male deficiency deficit.

Male deficiency deficit is an emotional vacuum that produces in the single woman a real craving for male companionship. The extent to which the woman feels this craving is proportionate to the extent of her past involvement with a man.

Sherry and Bob were married when they were in their late teens. Before his thirtieth birthday, Bob died of cancer leaving Sherry alone for the first time in here adult life. About a year after Bob died, Sherry began to experience feelings that were strange to her. She later explained these feelings as an emotional vacuum in her heart that craved for male companionship. However, before she figured out what she was feeling, Sherry had been exploited sexually by a friend of the family.

Male deficiency deficit is the kind of emotional vacuum that causes the single woman to be quite vulnerable. Thus, it is wise for the single woman to recognize that she has a genuine need for male companionship. Such acknowledgment will allow her to be on guard against emotional and sexual exploitation and will motivate her to seek healthy friendships with single men who just want to be a brother.

In this context of male deficiency deficit, I must add that the severe shortage of African-American men is likely to expand this problem unless the church involves itself more aggressively in the evangelization of African-American men in the social, religious and economic context where African-American men are to be found. This includes the prisons, the streets, the Islamic religion and drug rehabilitation centers.

In addition, the Christian community must do more to encourage fellowship between saved single men and women. This means having local and national meetings that are designed to bring together single men and women from all over the country for Christian fellowship with a view of establishing lasting friendships.

To marry a saved person who has no evident spiritual commitment is a difficult challenge in terms of making it work. To marry an unsaved person is genuine madness in terms of making a Christian home.

## MISINTERPRETING THE NEED

Shortage of available African-American men means that for a number of single women the option of dating is seriously limited. This also means that it is not unusual for a single woman not to have dated an African-American male for a period of several years.

This absence of male companionship over an extended period of time can cause single women to conclude that they have no need for male companionship. These women may also have a tendency to deny the reality of their natural sex drive.

This misconception often proves to be costly for the single woman's walk with God regarding moral behavior. It also results in an acquired insensitivity to natural desires that can render the woman morally vulnerable.

As a pastor, I have noted that moral failure in the lives of many Christian single women is the result of this acquired insensitivity. It appears that in such cases the single woman is in effect practicing her moral convictions in a social vacuum. The internal moral struggle is very real although it is often denied by some.

This leads to the question of whether a father's presence in the home is necessary for raising a child. A growing number of single women are saying no. This suggests that the shortage of African-American men is not only causing some single women to deny their need for male companionship, but they are also beginning to conclude that parenting without the father in the home is just as effective as it is with a father present.

For the Christian single the idea must be embraced that male and female companionship are essential to a balanced life and the idea of fatherhood means presence in the home. The single life does not necessarily mean living without male companionship. Single men and women can develop relationships that are morally pure and filled with companionship.

## A MAJOR DILEMMA

In contrast, the single African-American male is faced with what may best be described as an "over-population" of single women who often give the impression of being very available and sometimes very vulnerable. The African-American male is often made to feel as if he is a most precious commodity. Thus, for more than a few single adult males, choosing to maintain strong moral convictions often becomes a very serious struggle because there is the easy choice and open option to do that which their desires dictate. In other words the moral convictions of the African-American male are not practiced in a social vacuum as is often the case with the female.

This surplus of women plays well with the male's ability to initiate relationships while being less effective in nurturing and maintaining relationships. These relationships often remain in the initiation stage—seldom moving on into a formal commitment. The moral convictions of young African-American men are not lived in an external vacuum. They constantly face the challenge of maintaining moral purity on a daily basis.

On the other hand, the social context for the Christian female is very different in terms of her choice of the opposite sex as it pertains to dating, courting and marriage. She has too few choices for a potential mate. Thus, remaining single is not an option, but a probability. For some single African-American women, the idea of remaining single is not as much an issue, as is the possibility of never having the pleasure of sex and giving birth to their own children. Thus, the issue of artificial insemination is quite relevant as it relates to giving birth to their own children.

## A HIGH PRIORITY

At the same time it may well be said that the African-American male has too many choices in terms of his options as to who he will date, court and marry. Thus, some African-American men remain single just to enjoy the pleasure of being pursued by single women. In both instances the shortage of men for the African-American woman and the surplus of women for the African-American men becomes a challenge to the moral commitment for each one of them. Therefore, the need for discipleship and genuine spiritual commitment is a high priority for the African-American male and female.

This need for discipleship of singles must not be ignored by the church. To ignore the broad based spiritual needs of single Christians is to seriously diminish the resources of the Church. There are many social and economic circumstances in which a single person is best fitted for Christian service.

For most Christians, discipline in general is a problem. It is one of those things that we never really think much about, much less learn. All too often we are accustomed to getting what we want . . . when we want it. We live in a world where our society is quite undisciplined. Thus, when we encounter this command from God that we must abstain from sex outside of marriage, no matter our situation, we immediately have a problem. For, you see, such a principle is inconsistent with that to which we are accustomed. Yet, for the single Christian there must be the understanding that sexual purity is not only consistent with God's call of holiness upon our lives but is an essential part of a firm spiritual commitment. James was a very enthusiastic student of the word of God. He felt that he had his moral life well under control as a single adult in his mid-twenties. However, in many areas of his life, it was evident that James was not very disciplined. He often sought immediate self-gratification, even in his studies. This undisciplined temperament showed itself in James's moral life by way of masturbation. James was a frequent masturbator and in his mind there was nothing wrong with this habit.

What James needed was discipline through discipleship. This provided a context of accountability which caused him to overcome the problem of masturbation that also included lust and an eye for pornography.

## AN IMPORTANT DIFFERENCE

There is no such thing as sexual freedom in Christianity. In Christianity sex is confined to the marriage context. Yes, there are some church groups who have concluded that it is time to adopt a more liberal view of sex and the single person, but the Bible sharply disagrees with all such ideas. It is the role of the church to challenge the world to become more like it, rather than the church trying to become more like the world.

This new liberal attitude towards morality in the African-American church is both troubling and discouraging. In a time in which there is an alarming number of AIDS cases in the African-American community, a disproportionate number of illegitimate births and a growing commitment of African-American men to the Nation of Islam, the Christian church is increasingly adopting a more liberal attitude towards sexual morality. In the face of this softening, it is interesting to note that, in sharp contrast, the Nation of Islam is not adopting a liberal attitude towards sexual behavior among its members. The Nation of Islam is very conservative in its moral code as it pertains to sexual behavior. Thus, they take young African-American men off the streets and from the prisons and the inner cities (many of whom have a history of immoral activity) and bring them into the Islamic religion. Somehow they manage to rehabilitate these young people so that they become moral men and women.

The Nation of Islam does all this moral reforming in the lives of young African-American men and women without Christ. They focus exclusively on the will of the individual. I am sure they have failures among their converts, but the fact is they have a good rate of success. On the other hand, in our African-American churches immorality is all too often never spoken of from the pulpit. Young men and women are hardly ever challenged in this area of their sexual behavior. As a pastor for almost thirty years, I have had more than a few occasions in which I have had to deal in a disciplinary way with the problem of immorality in the church.

Some years ago I began a series of sermons on the subject of biblical morality. The series had six sermons, and I preached quite openly and frankly to the congregation about this issue of sexual immorality. About halfway through the series, one of the women in the church openly declared that if I mentioned the word *sex* one more Sunday, she was going to get up and walk out right in the middle of the sermon.

The sentiment of this woman was shared by a number of the women in the congregation at that time. What these woman did not know was that there were at least six young single girls in the church at the time who were pregnant, and several others who were sexually active.

As a young pastor, I discovered the hard way that preaching what the Bible says about sex and sexual behavior from the pulpit is uncomfortable for most church congregations, yet it must be done if we are going to grow moral Christians.

## THE NEED TO SPEAK OUT

I am convinced that the African-American church is far more equipped to challenge the moral behavior of its community than is the nonChristian Islamic religion of the Nation of Islam. We have the gospel of Jesus Christ and all of its inherent power. I argue, therefore, that the church must speak out boldly for abstinence, not safe sex, outside the context of marriage. It is a biblical absolute that must be obeyed by the church and strongly proclaimed by it.

I frequently find single Christian men and women who practice moral purity but who are somewhat ashamed to speak out about their commitment to biblical morality. It appears as if the moral climate even in the church is such that for Christians there is a sense in which abstinence from sexual immorality is so private that it must never be mentioned in public. This is an interesting attitude for Christians to have in a context in which immorality is the talk of every television talk show seen in prime time everyday.

We must make it clear that the Christian and the nonChristian single do not share a common view of sex and sexuality; and if and when they do, the motivation for their behavior is different. A Christian singles' view of sex and sexuality should be based on the view that every Christian must know how to possess his or her own body (vessel) in sanctification and honor. It is my view that the word *vessel* in 1 Thessalonians 4:3 is a reference to the human body and not to the wife (1 Pet. 3:7). To possess one's body in sanctification and honor in this context is to manage one's body with its external appeal and its internal passions in a way that honors God. To put it another way, Christians must have a lifestyle that is consistent with who they are as "new creations" in Christ Jesus (2 Cor. 5:17).

In our world today, however, emphasis is placed on sexual freedom. We constantly hear that the individual is free to express sexual desires in any way he pleases, with whomever he pleases, in any context in which he is comfortable, as long as the parties involved consent. This includes homosexual and bisexual activity. For many people, as it pertains to sex, the issue is "why not, if that is what you want to do?" Few people seem to realize that there is a downside to sexual freedom which is slavery to sexual involvement. Sexual freedom and the pleasure of sex may start out reigning together in a person's life. However, in short order, the pursuit of the pleasure of sex kills off the freedom to choose not to pursue sex, and makes the individual a slave to the pleasure of sex. Thus one must realize that their options are limited to total abstention from sex or enslavement to the pleasure of sex.

I am reminded of a salesperson who said to the customer regarding a certain product, "Try it, you just might like it." As it pertains to sex outside of marriage: "Don't try it, because you will like it."

## THE MYTH OF FREEDOM

Sexual freedom for the single adult is at best a dangerous myth. It is my contention that in marriage the pleasure of sex holds a significant number of marriages together. I believe to "do sex" is to become addicted to its pleasure. This is why many of our single people have child after child out of wedlock. They are addicted to the pleasure inherent in the experience.

Though there may be some poor women who have child after child just to increase their welfare check, it is more likely that most poor single women, as well as middle class single women have one goal in mind: sexual gratification. We can hardly make the argument that sexual immorality is the pursuit of pleasure among the middle class but greed among the poor. The fact is the pursuit of sexual pleasure knows no economic boundaries.

To be consistent with their Christian commitment, single Christians, regardless of their economic status, must reject the idea of so-called sexual freedom, choosing rather to learn how to manage their own bodies in sanctification and honor. This means acknowledging the fact that because they are single Christians, they are unable to fully express their sexual desires. This does not mean they do not have sexual desires, nor does it mean that they do not struggle with those desires. The Christian singles' moral distinction is not that they do not have sexual desires the same as the unsaved. The Christian and the unsaved share a common biological need in which sexual desires are a part of what it means to be a healthy, mature adult. How the Christian manages his/her desires is the distinction. The Christian must understand that sexual desires are not in themselves evil. The point, however, is that how those desires are expressed will either honor or dishonor God.

Jean is a divorcée and her children are grown. For the past years, Jean has been going it alone, living for the Lord and being extensively involved in the local church ministry. Jean's testimony as a single woman in the area of morality is impeccable; yet she will quickly tell you that the thing she misses as a single divorcée is the pleasure of intimacy. As she contemplates her future, she is saddened by the prospect of not having the option to marry again and experience the pleasure of intimacy again.

I have found that more than a few women are a bit uncomfortable with Jean's openness about her feeling in this area. Yet it seems to me that it is this kind of attitude that is the strength of her celibate lifestyle.

Yvette was always very attractive. Even as a young girl her beauty was evident and she developed into a very beautiful young woman. Today, Yvette is single in her mid-thirties and has several children—each by a different man. In conversation with Yvette, one quickly comes to understand that as a single woman who is also a mother, one of her major struggles is with the pleasure of sex. Thus, in spite of the consequences of having yet another child by a different man, she inevitably succumbed even after abstaining for up to two years.

As a pastor, one of my strong arguments against a young person becoming sexually active outside the context of marriage is the power of the pleasure of sex in the life of the one who participates in it. I often say with a bit of comedy that sex is much like a good potato chip—nobody can have just one.

We need to keep in mind that one of the clearest differences that distinguishes the Christian single from the unsaved in this matter is how they think about sex and conduct themselves socially and morally. It seems to me that it is wise to be on guard against the trap of the pleasure of sex and the inherent power of that pleasure in the life of any individual.

## RECOGNIZING THE DIFFERENCE

Moral purity that is consistent with one's Christian commitment means understanding the difference between normal sexual desires and lustful passions. Moral sexual desires are best defined as the natural biological and emotional manifestations of hormones in which there is an attraction to the opposite sex. It is a desire for both the pleasure of intimacy and the joy of reproduction. I can remember when my son disdained the very idea of a girl being attracted to him much less his being attracted to a girl. However, as he matured in years what was once disgusting to him increasingly became a strong motivating force in his life. The more he grew towards adulthood, the more he treasured the idea of female companionship.

Adulthood for most healthy men and women means having sexual as well as other desires for the opposite sex. The biblical idea is that these desires are best fully expressed in the context of a relationship with an individual to whom you are bonded in marriage. Lust, on the other hand, is a focus on the pleasure of sex, apart from the commitment of marriage which involves a commitment to the individual. Lust is a focus on pleasure, not people.

For the unsaved, their sexual appetite controls both their attitude and their moral behavior towards the opposite sex. It is the belief of the unsaved that sexual freedom is the "in" thing. The only restraint is one's own choice in the matter. On the other hand, the saved single's sexual desires are controlled by his/her spiritual contentment. The saved person is committed to honoring God with body, mind and spirit. To put it another way, the primary distinction between the sexual attitude of the saved and unsaved is control and conduct, not the presence or absence of sexual desires. Even though both the saved and the unsaved share the same biology, they are very different in how they manage those desires.

As it pertains to moral purity, the Lord instructs Christians not to allow their desires to dictate their conduct. "Not in lustful passions like the pagans do who do not know God" (1 Thess. 4:5). In the mind of God, the Christian and the nonChristian do not share a common moral belief. Thus, as it pertains to dating, entertainment, socializing, and education, the Christian world view is recognizably different from that of the unsaved.

## AVOID THE PITFALLS

In order to maintain moral purity, the single Christian must choose a social lifestyle that is not sexually stimulating or seducing. This means being willing to screen movies, literature and social functions which are acceptable to you as a Christian and with which you as a single adult will allow yourself to get involved. It means that you will choose dates who share your moral convictions and who will not seek to sexually arouse you. It means avoiding such things as petting because it arouses sexual desires and turns them into lust which demands fulfillment.

Immorality disrupts the Christian's progressive sanctification, thus God's purpose for the Christian is also disrupted; and in some instances, God's purpose is wiped out in their lives. Since such is the case, it must be understood that to reject God's teaching about immorality is much the same as rejecting God.

Since this is the case, I must challenge any Christian who is today practicing immorality to cease such activity and repent of that sin right now. You will find that living with moral purity with all of its struggles is much more satisfying than living with the guilt of moral sin in your life.

# CHAPTER 3

# THE DANGER OF TRYING TO HELP GOD OUT

A major struggle faced by a number of Christians is maintaining faith and confidence in the promises of God when time and circumstances seem to be running in the opposite direction. This struggle is no less true in the lives of single African-American women in many areas of their lives, but especially as it pertains to marriage before they reach a certain age. There is a generally held conviction in the Black community that the single woman who does not marry and have children by a certain age will forever be single and childless.

This widely held view that a woman must enter marriage by a certain age combined with the promises of God to provide an abundant life for all sheep of His pasture often contributes to single women getting involved in relationships that can only be defined as "Trying to Help God Out."

Over the years in the pastorate I have had dozens of cases in which the relationship between two professing Christians was initiated by one or both of them as an effort on their part to help God fulfill His promise to meet their need of a Christian mate. In their attempt to help God do His thing in their lives these believers enter into a courtship and subsequently a marriage relationship without any consideration of the differences and difficulties that they faced in their courtship. These problems ultimately showed up in their marriage.

In Genesis 16, we have a case in which two God-fearing saints got caught in the struggle between faith, circumstances and the promise of God. The choices

Abraham and his wife Sarah made in this struggle of faith, in which they tried to help God out, hundreds of years ago is evident in our day in the hostile relationship between Arabs and Jews.

## GOD'S PROMISES REQUIRE FAITH

In considering the idea: "The danger of trying to help God out," I think it is appropriate to focus on it through the experience of Abraham, his wife Sarah, and their maid Hagar. This view is in the context of the experience of Abraham and his wife Sarah's response to God's promise to give them a son in their old age.

To begin with, Abraham's conduct with Hagar, Sarah's maid, was not a reflection of any lack of faith on his part in believing the promise of God. For we are told that Abraham did not waver at the promise of God (Rom. 4:20). "And being fully assured, that what He, [God], had promised, He was able also to perform" (v. 21). Clearly from these verses we are to understand that God's promise to give him a son in spite of their ages through whom He, God, would build a nation, was received by Abraham with unwavering faith in that promise. In other words unbelief was not Abraham's problem; therefore, it could not have dictated Abraham's conduct with Hagar.

In order to get at the problem that precipitated Abraham and Sarah's conduct with the maid, Hagar, a few facts must be considered. First, Abraham, in spite of his faith had in times past for the sake of expedience, found it necessary to lie to pagan kings regarding his relationship to Sarah. In two different instances Abraham said that Sarah was his sister instead of his wife (Gen. 13:12ff; Gen. 19:1ff.). In this situation Abraham practiced situational ethics. The fact was whatever else Sarah was to Abraham, she was also his wife.

Second, about 16 years had come and gone since God had promised to give Abraham a son and Abraham was 86 years old—hardly the age of high fertility. Sarah being 76 years old, was several years beyond the possibility of reproduction.

These two factors in Abraham's life, provided a foundation for his attempt at helping God out. A third factor that might be considered is the absence of specific revelation regarding the mother of the son in the promise made by God. Recalling for a moment Abraham's conduct with the King of Egypt regarding his relationship with Sarah, Abraham felt it necessary to lie to protect his life rather than trust the Lord. This to some extent at least, was a compromise of his integrity that involved situational ethics, or to put it another way, this was Abraham's way of helping God out.

Some sixteen years had elapsed since the promise had been made. We must recognize that while the passing of time did not diminish Abraham's faith, it pushed their emotions to the point of frustration and feelings of desperation. They felt a need for examining the promise God had made to them with a view to checking the details of how this son would be given. As they examined the specifics of the promise they noted that there was nothing in the promise that specified the name of the promised son's mother.

Thus being a man of faith, totally committed to the promise God had made to him, it must have seemed reasonable to Abraham and his wife that Hagar could possibly be the promised son's mother. After all the promise was to Abraham and his seed. Sarah was way past the years of fertility, but her maid Hagar was not.

Abraham and Sarah, like most Christians through the years, must have struggled with their own perception of how God was going to accomplish this impossible promise of giving them a son in their old age. They tried to make sense of their situation with God, in view of their biological limitations. In their struggle to intellectually get a hold on this promise God had made to them, they overlooked the fact that faith in God, no matter what the promise may be, most often presents to the object of the promise what is in most cases an irrational and illogical situation.

As Abraham and his wife Sarah struggled to give action to their faith, they came to what must have been to them, a logical and reasonable means of bringing to fruition God's promise of a son to them. Sarah decided to give her maid Hagar, to her husband Abraham for the night, for the express purpose of conceiving God's promised seed in the form of a son.

This action on the part of Abraham and his wife Sarah, was a reflection of their willingness to compromise godly conviction and moral standards when circumstances seemed to be a threat to the fulfillment of God's promise. This spirit of compromise on their part combined with their unwavering faith in God's promise, provided the ingredients for Abraham and Sarah's feeble attempt at helping God out.

When believers try to help God out, most often they create for themselves the kind of trouble that scars their lives forever. This trouble often spills over into the lives of others causing conflict.

## Caught in the Trap of an Illusion of Happiness

Being confident that he and Sarah had found a way to accomplish or bring to fruition God's promise through the impregnation of Sarah's maid Hagar, Abraham must have been happy and excited about the prospect of having his firstborn—God's promised seed.

According to their plan, through the impregnation of Hagar—Abraham, Sarah, and God had fulfilled God's promise of a son. This means that they had accomplished God's plan for their lives.

It is often the case that what Christians do in the flesh, under the umbrella of logic and reason, seems not only to be right and consistent with faith, but also most often is thought to be what is best for everybody involved. Such was the case with Abraham and Sarah. They thought they had found a way to accomplish God's will in their lives. They thought this plan was best for Hagar also. However, such is seldom the case.

Abraham's involvement with Hagar was not of long duration. Her impregnation was most likely immediate. Thus Abraham and his wife Sarah, were sincerely seeking to accomplish the will of God in their lives but instead, inadvertently fell into the trap of trying to help God out. Good people tend to do this all the time as a means of accommodating their faith.

So many times in the Christian community contractual agreements are made in business, ministry, and marriage that are aimed at accomplishing God's will and fulfilling His promise. They are in reality attempts at helping God out.

Many Christians who sincerely try to help God out ultimately find themselves living in the illusion of happiness. They convince themselves that they are happy in their situation because they participated in producing a desired situation. In reality, however, the situation is most unpleasant.

We must understand that it's almost always possible for us to get what we want if we want it bad enough and are willing to do whatever is necessary to get it. However, we must not make the mistake of thinking that because we get what we want or are where we want to be, we have accomplished His will in our lives.

We must always be reminded that we can beg God for something, and He will allow us to get what we want, but having it will grieve our very souls. It's also possible to manipulate our way into things from which we can not be easily extricated. I find an increasing number of people who live in what I call the illusion of happiness. They have resigned themselves to living in the mess they have created and pretend to be happy.

You see, just because you get what you want when you want it does not mean that what you get will make you happy. You may work your thing and get your way—but will it make you happy? You may get the best job, the prettiest woman or the most handsome man— but will it make you happy? The person who lays hold of God's promise is one who is willing to let God fulfill His promise in His time . . . in His way.

I think that the notion that God helps those who help themselves is a deadly notion for the Christian. For every Christian must know that without and apart from the enabling power of God, we can do nothing. We must also understand that we are not smart enough to help ourselves in most situations. Surely we are not smart enough to help God do His thing. For indeed most of what we do for ourselves seem right in our own eyes but all too often the end thereof is disaster.

This illusory state of happiness based on getting what one desires is as true of men as it is of women. Both feign happiness if they wed the desired person, obtain longed for material possessions, or visit sites they have dreamed about.

While Abraham and Sarah were rejoicing in success in fulfilling God's will in their lives, pride sprang up in the heart of Hagar and gave birth to a contentious spirit towards her mistress Sarah. Hagar was proud that she had become in effect what amounted to Abraham's wife. Being pregnant and in this frame of mind, she began to resent Abraham's real wife. Sarah was also mocked by Hagar because she was too old to get pregnant. To put this is street language Hagar, Abraham's woman of convenience began to feel that she was his main woman. Sarah was not about to stand for that.

This strife between Sarah and Hagar got so bad that Sarah had to exercise her authority and have Abraham throw Hagar out of the house. This action shattered their illusion of happiness evidencing the futility of trying to help God out. Most of the time when we try to help God out somebody gets hurt.

## THE DANGER OF TRYING TO HELP GOD OUT

Any attempt at helping God out is like the process of generating electricity through a nuclear plant. There is no safe way to handle the waste material that is the by-product of nuclear generated electricity. So it is with the by product of the efforts of sincere believers who try to help God out. There is no safe method of dealing with the shattered lives that result from such efforts.

In this instance Hagar was the by-product of Abraham and Sarah's efforts to help God accomplish His will in their lives. Hagar in this situation was the disposable product of good people attempting to do God's thing their way, according to their sense of timing.

It became evident that the impregnation of Hagar was after all not the best idea or even a good idea, and certainly not God's idea. This was evidenced by Hagar's proud and arrogant attitude. Sarah deduced that Hagar was the problem, not what they had done to her. So Sarah sought to rid herself of the problem by disposing of Hagar the victim. To accomplish her goal to get rid of Hagar, Sarah began to treat her cruelly and eventually threw her out of the house.

When we try to help God out, we ought to count on producing victims. In this text it is evident that there was no one to whom Sarah could send Hagar, and she had no family to whom she could return. Christians who involve themselves in futile efforts to help God do His thing in their lives are often found in the dilemma of trying to conceal the debris that results from such efforts. In this situation, Hagar was such debris in the lives of the God-fearing family of Abraham and Sarah.

Now pregnancy is known to be for most single women in particular, a lonely and sometimes frightening experience. Given how things had turned out for Hagar, I would imagine that if one had met Hagar after she had been thrown out of Sarah's house and left to wander in the desert, and asked her how she felt, she might have replied, "I feel like a loose strand of hair in a wig factory." She might have said, "I feel like a broken doll, in a doll factory." Pressed for a further explanation of her feeling she might have added, "I feel like a gum wrapper in a garbage truck on its way to the dump ground." I take it that as a by-product of Sarah's spiritual folly, Hagar felt like nothing, wrapped up in nobody, on her way to nowhere.

Unfortunately, I have met and ministered to no small number of single women in particular who were caught in situations like Hagar's. These women and some men were victims of believers who knew and believed the promises of God as it pertained to their particular situation. In an effort to accommodate their faith they dared to try and help God do what He had promised in their lives.

The point I am making is that when you try to help God out somebody always gets hurt, and sometimes the hurt is irreparable. Furthermore, when we attempt to help God out we create situations that neither time nor circumstances can change.

There is an alternative to helping God out which is: believe that what God has promised, He is also able to fulfill. Neither time nor circumstances are hindrances to God fulfilling His promise. There is no need for us to try and help Him do what He promised.

I heard the story of a young single mother of two small children who was fired from her job. She sought a new job but lost out to another applicant for the same job. In desperation and despair the young mother of two took her life obviously concluding that there was no hope for her. About a week after she had killed herself, the union got her old job back.

Wait on the Lord! "I waited patiently for the Lord; and He inclined to me, and heard my cry. He brought me up out of the pit of destruction out of the miry clay. And He set my feet upon a rock making my footsteps firm" (Ps. 40).

# CHAPTER 4

# THE PERFECT SIN

Masturbation is defined as any kind of sexual self-stimulation that leads to erotic arousal in which orgasm is a frequent though not necessarily essential result. According to some experts in the field of human sexuality, masturbation is a common sexual activity among both males and females. It is alleged that upwards to 90 percent of men and 60 percent of all women masturbate at some point in their lives. Among both married and single people, masturbation is perceived to be the quickest and most successful method of achieving an orgasm.

In the world of secular human sexuality, masturbation is perceived to be a normal sexual activity contributing in a positive way to the development of sensual capacity. Masturbation is said to be a common practice among young adults, old adults, young children and adolescents. However, mental health professionals both secular and Christian discourage such practice as the only outlet for sexual pleasure.

When my son, now sixteen, was entering his teens, he and I had one of our many conversations about sex and sexuality. In one conversation about sexual intercourse, moral purity and such, I observed that he was using words like "nutting" and "choking the chicken." For a while I was at a loss in understanding what it was that he was talking about. I asked him the meaning of the words that he was using. As I listened to his explanation of what he meant, I immediately recognized that he was speaking of masturbation. As a father, I decided that my son like many sons of Christian and nonChristian parents, will most likely in his adolescence experiment with masturbation. For me, a Christian father, that is acceptable. I am one of those fathers who thinks that nocturnal emissions (wet dreams) and masturbation are a part of growing up into a healthy man. While as a father, I have no objection to the kind of childhood activity that leads to masturbation in adolescence. As an experienced pastor and counselor, however, I have seen the ugly destructive results of what happens when masturbation is a habit in an adult male.

I call the habit of masturbation "the perfect sin," because it is private; it is secretive; it involves no one but the individual who has the habit. I have not known masturbation to become a habit with women. I am sure it does, but I am not able to speak to that at this point except to say that the same principle stated for men applies equally to women with the same habit.

When masturbation becomes a habit like any other habit, it has the power to completely control that person's life. The habit of masturbation is the product of a fertile imagination focused on sexual things. Thus the habitual masturbator is usually also hooked on pornography; in fact, the habitual masturbator has the uncanny ability to turn any picture of a woman or any part of female apparel into something pornographic.

The habitual masturbator is not only usually hooked on pornography, he is also normally given to strong lustful passions that can only be fulfilled with pornography and masturbation. The Christian man who is hooked on masturbation is a man loaded down with guilt feelings about his habit. This secret habit causes him to feel like a phony in his Christian commitment. The habit of masturbation is to the Christian masturbator a powerful raging monster always lurking in the dark corridors of his fertile sexual imagination.

In dealing with the habit of masturbation for a while, I was of the opinion that marriage would solve the problem. Much to my surprise that is not the case. In many instances the habitual masturbator continues on a regular basis his habit of masturbating in addition to his intimacy with his wife. Marriage does not solve this problem.

I discovered that the power that masturbation holds over its victims is in the secret nature of the habit. The reason masturbation is a perfect sin is because it is the kind of sin that is possible to keep entirely secret even from one's wife.

Men who have the habit of masturbating are usually into serious denial as it pertains to the degree to which this sin has power over their lives. They will compare themselves to others and conclude that they are not really hooked on the practice. They want to believe that they can quit the practice any time they want. The fact is that they are most always much worse off than they will admit; they cannot quit. The power of this sin is in the secret nature of the sin.

Ben and Mary had a big wedding and went on their honeymoon to begin their lifetime commitment to each other. After a few days of marriage, Mary noticed that Ben was not really entering into the intimacy she was experiencing. When she questioned Ben about this, she discovered that he was a habitual masturbator; the real pleasure of sex for Ben was in pornography and masturbation. To say the least, Mary was crushed. She thought something was wrong with her.

The fact was that Ben's problem had nothing to do with Mary. Ben would have responded to any woman just as he responded to his wife Mary. Masturbation is the kind of habit that feeds on itself; actual sexual intercourse does nothing to satisfy its demands.

The habitual masturbator is usually a man who grew up in a family in which sex and sexuality was treated as something less than normal. There was probably a double standard, one public and the other private, as it pertains to sexual attitudes and behavior. For instance, in the case of Ben and Mary, Ben's father was a church deacon who publicly preached fidelity and morality, but who privately practiced infidelity with prostitutes. Ben grew up knowing this about his father.

To deal with the problem of masturbation, the first order of business is to come out of your secret room and make the problem public. The power of the habit of masturbation is in the secret nature of the practice; thus to break the habit the man must go public with the problem. The second thing the masturbator should do is make himself accountable to a significant somebody or join a group of men who are recovering from the same problem. Third, to break the habit of masturbation the man must memorize Scripture as a mean of cleansing his mind.

The guilt of masturbation is a serious problem in that it robs the man of his dignity as a child of God. It sets him up for catastrophic failure in every area of his life, beginning with marriage and later in his ministry.

To avoid the problem of habitual masturbation, every boy needs to have access to a healthy sex education. This education in my opinion is best taught by the father or some other Christian man. The discussions about sex and sexuality with boys need to be open and frank; every effort should be made to keep sexual attitudes and behavior from becoming a closet issue. The power of masturbation is that it is a closet habit.

I have spent nearly a quarter of a century of my life on a graduate school campus where the majority of the students are single Christian men. In this environment it is not uncommon to discover that masturbation is a common practice. However, I am of the opinion that not many of the men who practice masturbation have any idea how powerful and how potentially destructive this practice can be should it become a habit. For many it is a habit that they have yet to acknowledge.

I encourage single men who have strong public moral convictions to be sure to deal with masturbation as a potentially life controlling adversary. I do not say don't do it, I say if you choose to do this, be forewarned that you are playing with a destructive force that is always present in your life as a man, single or married.

CHAPTER 5

# THE CURE FOR
# SPIRITUAL FAILURE

---

While sitting in my office I heard a knock at the door that was soft but persistent. I thought for a while that it was one of the children passing by to say "hi" to the pastor. I said, "Come in." After a brief hesitation the door opened and in stepped a young man seriously burdened about his walk with God. This young man was saved after going through two marriages and a serious alcohol problem. He had been walking with the Lord and doing quite well until the weekend that he got involved in a situation that lead to his drinking heavily and forfeiting his testimony before his friends.

As I visited with him about his spiritual failure, I realized that he had been overtaken in a fault (Gal. 6:1) and he decided to share his struggle with his pastor. We sat together in my office and talked and prayed about his situation. As we prayed together I was thankful again for God's marvelous provision of grace and forgiveness. There are times when believers face spiritual failure.

For more than thirty years I have spent a great deal of my time listening to Christians pray in a variety of settings, including church, conventions, hospitals and homes. When Christians pray in any of these settings they tend to thank God for all sorts of things including food, friends, jobs and family. Seldom do I hear Christians express gratitude to God for that great and marvelous provision: the forgiveness of our sins. If that for which a person expresses gratitude is a reflection of what that person considers to be a blessing, then it could be concluded that for many Christians forgiveness of sins is not considered to be a significant blessing.

I have seen people who prayed when they were sick and thanked God for healing. Often I hear people testify to answered prayer for a job or for their children. In all of these situations Christians express strong gratitude to God for hearing and answering their prayers. With this in mind, how do we as Christians explain the silence of believers on the issue of forgiveness of sins? Could it be that we no longer recognize our need for forgiveness and no longer confess our sins to the living God? Have we reached such a high point in our philosophy of spiritual nurture which includes such things as spiritual formation groups, cell groups, support groups, and a wide variety of Christian counseling groups that sin and forgiveness are no longer relevant to the Christian life? Has the church become so caught up in the verbal and emotional calisthenics of praise, worship, and spiritual gifts that it has lost sight of the reality of individual sin and the need for personal forgiveness? Are we as the people of God prepared to proclaim that we have achieved the impossible task of becoming holy and righteous without being conscious of the oppressiveness of sin and the blessedness of forgiveness?

Quite frankly, I find it strange and even a bit frightening to see in the church a people unconscious of the need and blessedness of forgiveness while being stricken with all the symptoms of the burden of sin and the absence of forgiveness. If more than three decades of ministry among singles of all ages and both genders have taught me anything, it is that the greatest need and the greatest blessing for both saint and sinner alike is the need for and the experience of forgiveness of sin. Apart from this experience, the emotional and psychological impact of the guilt sin produces in the uncalloused conscience of Christians has the power to drive that person to physical and emotional ruin.

When it comes to spiritual failure the Christian has one of three choices: repeat the sin frequently enough so that the voice of the Holy Spirit is silenced; live with the pain and shame that sin produces; get rid of the guilt and agony of the sin through forgiveness.

In Psalm 32, the Psalmist speaks to the issue of the blessedness of forgiveness in the context of spiritual failure. It is good to be reminded that sin, no matter the specific offense involved, is ultimately against God. Thus it can be concluded that whenever a believer sins there is an instant loss of fellowship with God, which can only be restored by confession and forgiveness.

The Psalmist employs three different terms to express the content of the believer's struggle with sin which often leads to spiritual failure.The first is *transgression* which means a violation of and rebellion against God's word. Second, *sin* which refers here to conduct that deliberately misses or falls short of God's standard and or purpose. Third, *iniquity* which means turning away from God in perverseness.

In reading this Psalm one gets the impression that the Psalmist lived in the real world of spiritual struggle like Christians today. Living as he did in the real world of spiritual struggle, the Psalmist sets forth the idea that the truly blessed person is that man or woman, single or married, old or young, who experiences the divine grace manifested in and through the forgiveness of sin and the removal of the guilt that accompanies sin.

We know what is meant by spiritual failure and the guilt of sin. We might not know what is meant by forgiveness of sin and the removal of the guilt thereof. Forgiveness in any context depicts sin and its consequences as a burden which can be lifted and carried away. The burden of sin is a guilty conscience that cannot be silenced for long no matter the effort or the method employed. This burden of sin can only be lifted by God's forgiveness, which the believer must accept.

The Psalmist says that the blessedness of forgiveness includes the covering of the sin by God who forgives. To cover the believer's sins in this context of Christian living is pictured as the covering of that which is offensive in the eye of the living God so that He is no longer compelled to act restitutionally in response to the believer's sin.

The idea that God has covered with the blood of Jesus all the sins of believers should be sufficient grounds for the believer to reject all manner of counseling that uncovers and reviews the sins that God has covered over with the blood of Jesus.

In the blessedness of forgiveness is also the truth that God does not impute sin to the believer. This means that God's forgiveness does not credit to the spiritual account of the believer those sins that are confessed and forgiven.

I have sought to make the point that for the person who sins and experiences the subsequent feelings of guilt, anxiety and such, there is available to such a one divine deliverance which removes, covers, and cancels all the spiritual and emotional consequences of that act. In the context of the spiritual life in which there is persistent struggle to live for the Lord, the Christian must know that there is the great blessing of forgiveness whenever there is spiritual failure. This Psalm illustrates what happens when the believer chooses not to confess his or her, sins thereby foregoing the blessedness of forgiveness.

The believer who sins and decides not to confess that sin (choosing rather to hide the sin), is plunged into depression from which deliverance is nonexistent—even with the best of therapy. This is what I call the grieving of the Holy Spirit. Believers who have unconfessed sin in their lives will discover that their bodies and emotions are affected by the consequences.

Even though believers act as if forgiveness for sin is not something for which they should be publicly grateful, they are nonetheless stricken with all the internal and external symptoms of unconfessed sin. Depression is perhaps the most vivid expression of the result of unconfessed sin in the life of a Christian. I am fully aware that there are many different causes of depression in Christians. Yet, it must be said that among those many causes, unconfessed sin is a major one.

Sin tucked away in the emotional closet of a Christian will rob that believer's body of its physical strength. The body in which the mind is laden with the burden of guilt from unconfessed sins will waste away losing its stamina. Sin left unconfessed in the life of a Christian has the power to steal both the youth and the vigor of that believer. Such a person is always tired and filled with anxiety. Living in spiritual failure means living the kind of life in which the hand of God is ever upon the unrepentant Christian, pressing him/her to the point of exhaustion. They are not able to relax, sleep well, be at peace or experience real joy.

Unfortunately, I find this profile of the unrepentant all too often among Christians. The church is ever encompassed about with a group of people who are too tired to get up, too rested to go to sleep, too bored to be comfortable, too miserable to be happy and yet they claim no need for forgiveness because they admit to no spiritual failure. In all too many cases the problem is the problem of unconfessed sin. There is no drug on the market that can cure the problem of unconfessed sin. The only cure is God's blessed forgiveness.

The cure for spiritual failure is nothing less than confession to God. The Psalmist said, "I acknowledged my sin to the Lord and I did not hide my perverse conduct from Him" (32:5). I take it that the only way to deal with depression produced by unconfessed sin is to confess the sin or sins. No psychiatrist, no doctor, and no medicine in all the world can cure the sin problem—only confession of sin can do that.

When the Psalmist said, "I will confess my transgressions " I take it that the Psalmist is referring here to his willful violation and rebellion against the Law of God. Confession involves genuine repentance, which is a complete change of attitude towards the wrong done. It involves giving up all forms of rationalization and excuses as to why you did what you did. It means coming to the point at which you simply say: I did it; it was wrong. When in repentance we confess our sin, God always forgives the sin.

CHAPTER 6

# MAINTAINING A CLEAN LIFE IN A DIRTY WORLD

I do not profess to be an authority on human behavior; I do not have credentials in the field of the behavioral sciences. My credentials are in the field of theology and pastoral ministries. However, I do feel competent, based on more than thirty years of ministry to concur with those behavioral specialists who say that people are creatures of habit. I contend that nurture is the key ingredient in determining what a person learns as a child and ultimately becomes as an adult. Thus, I argue that parents should strive to create and maintain the best environment possible in which to grow their children into adults. I believe people become what they are taught to be.

It does not require the perception of a prophet nor does it necessitate the wisdom of a philosopher to realize that the world in which we live is not nor will it ever be an ideal environment conducive to producing people who are inherently positive and persistently productive. Our world seems to be designed to produce people who are given to violence and self-destruction.

The transmission of the values of our race, the integrity that for years has characterized Black people in America and the moral standards that are the legacy of the oppressed African-American, have in this day been abandoned by the custodians of the African-American culture. These values are then left to be transmitted to our children by advertising agencies whose primary goal is making money by selling products and ideas that exploit the African-American community.

The artists and entertainers of today including those who are themselves African-American, are peddling spiritual, moral, social and economic pollution. Many of our young artists are in reality flawed with the pollution of that which is immoral. It can be seen or heard in their movies, music, and comedy routines. And yet these are the people who are all to often the transmitters of the values of our community.

I have entitled this section "How to Keep a Clean Life in a Dirty World." I have in view here the principle set forth in Philippians 4:8: "Whatever is true, whatever is honorable, whatever is right, whatever is pure, whatever is of good repute, if there is any excellence and if anything worthy of praise, let your mind dwell on these things."

I am concerned today about the moral pollution of the minds of Christians. Our culture is increasingly filled with that which is neither pure, right or excellent. One of the most popular television sitcoms, *Martin* portrays the stars of the show living together without being married. The African-American movie and music producers have labeled the young Black woman "bitch" and made it stick. The young African-American rappers have become as "nasty as they want to be" and made it acceptable. It is in this context that I raise the issue of maintaining a clean life in a dirty world.

People are creatures of habit. We learn everything we believe and do. Therefore, it must be concluded that what we are exposed to in the context of our nurturing will have the greatest impact on the kind of adult we become. With this in mind, consider the extensive exposure children, teens and single adults have to television and music. These media have in fact become the primary teachers and trendsetters of values and moral principles of our day.

The question that we must face is this: "How is it possible to maintain a clean life in this our dirty world?" In seeking an answer to this question a growing number of young African-Americans do not have the option of turning to their fathers; their fathers are not around. They cannot find the answer in contemporary music and literature; it has given over to that which is often degrading, frequently self-aggrandizing, and self-destructive. We seem to be surrounded by people who are confused and filled with anxiety. Thus, like a voice echoing in the back alleys of a dark slum community, the question keeps on ringing out: "How can I live a clean life in this dirty world?"

In Psalm 119:9-16, there is an answer to this question. To live a clean life in a dirty world the believer must acknowledge that living the Christian life is a struggle that involves both hills and valleys.. The believer who is in the valley today may be on the hill tomorrow and vise versa. For many Christians this means acknowledging that their life is in need of the grace of God that delivers from sin and fixes that which is broken. To put it another way—many Christians need to say this to the Lord: "Lord, my life is crooked, dirty, polluted with sin and sinfulness; I need you to fix it."

Living a clean life in a dirty world also means knowing and memorizing the Word of God combined with a commitment to obey the Word of God. In this context let me say that there are a number of devotional books, self-help books, motivational books, and tapes written by fine godly men and women. However, these resource materials, as good as they may be, are not sufficient when it comes to straightening out a messed up spiritual life and then maintaining a clean life in a dirty world.

There are many good schools to which believers can go and gain much in the field of their choice. Education cannot straighten a crooked life, nor can it enable the Christian to maintain a clean life in a dirty world. Maintaining a clean life in a dirty world demands hiding the Word of God in the heart (Ps. 119:11). That word will keep the life of the believer clean.

Religion is good and profitable for most. There are few if any cultures in the world in which religion of some form is not a part of that culture. However, religion as good as it may be, cannot fix a broken life nor can it empower and equip a person with that which is necessary to maintain a clean life in a dirty world. Only the Word of God in the human heart can do that.

The Psalmist tells us in verse 14 that he rejoiced in the way of God's testimony as much as in all riches. God's testimonies are those principles set forth in the Scriptures that contain God's standard of righteousness and His faithfulness. The Scriptures are a faithful and true witness to God and His dealings with man. This knowledge of God is the beginning of wisdom which leads to living a clean life in a dirty world.

For the Psalmist, knowing what to do to please God as well as what not to do to offend God, were equal in importance to having great wealth. The Psalmist knew that those who chose to wrap their ideas of success and happiness with the polluted covers of the values of this world were doomed to a life of vanity. But those who chose not to walk in the counsel of the wicked nor stand in the sin polluted path of sinners or sit in the seat of scoffers were those who were truly blessed (Ps. 1:1). According to the Psalmist, avoiding the path that is polluted with sin demands that the believer hide the word of God in his or her heart. "Thy word I have hid in my heart that I might not sin against thee" (Ps. 119:11).

I began this section by making the case that this world as we know it, is not, nor will it ever be a place that is ideal for growing healthy adults. However, since this is the only world we have to grow up and live in, we must find a means by which we can develop a positive and productive attitude and life-style. This means finding a source from which we can obtain something to filter out the values of this world thus freeing us up to live a clean life in this dirty world.

The key to developing and maintaining a clean life in this dirty world is the Word of God stored in our heart. The Word of God is the only defense we have against sin. Knowing better than to do wrong will not keep the Christian from doing the wrong they know better than to do. Fear of the consequences of sin will not keep the believer from doing wrong. It is often easy to conclude that the pleasure of sin is worth the pain of the consequences. Intellectualism and strong cultural commitments will not prevent an attraction to sin. Many of the most cultured people we know are among the most evil. To keep a clean life in a dirty world, the Word of God stored in the human heart is the only thing that works in every situation, whether single or married, old or young, male or female.

It is obvious from Psalm 119:9-16 that the Word of God in its entirety is for the Christian the source and resource for spiritual growth. The Word of God must be the object of serious study. Verse 10 focuses on serious conversation centered on the Word of God; verse 13 addresses the substance of quiet meditation which should be on the Word of God; and verse 15 deals with the foundation of life's success and delight which is the Word of God.

The Bible teaches us a number of things that are essential to our spiritual growth: who God is, who we are, why we are here, love, marriage, family life, truth, justice, freedom, eternity, sin and righteousness.

It is important to understand from the Word of God that there are only two eternal things on this earth, namely the Word of God and the souls of people. Everything else is temporal. It seems to me then that our behavior ought to reflect this fact.

# CHAPTER 7

# IT AIN'T LOVE . . . IT'S LUST

Life for most singles is quite exciting because it is filled with challenges and opportunities to be involved in a variety of ministries and social activities. The idea that being single is boring and disappointing is not at all true when reflected through the eyes of many single men and women.

While there are a number of single men and women who are enjoying their single life unencumbered, there is a group of singles who seem to have been tossed into the arena of single adulthood prematurely. I speak here of a growing number of teenage boys and girls who are involved in serious courtships often before their sixteenth birthday. For these premature adults the single life is most difficult and confusing

Courtship is the kind of relationship that should be reserved for those men and women who plan to be married within a period of time. Thus courtship is reserved for adults only. A major problem with premature courtship is that most teens are ill-equipped emotionally, spiritually, and intellectually to distinguish between love and lust. There is a difference, and unfortunately when most teens discover the difference they have already made decisions that have negatively affected their lives.

In my years of experience as a pastor and counselor I have observed that there are a number of ways men and women, boys and girls come together and form relationships. I have also observed that the thing that brings a couple together contributes to the nature of the relationship over a period of time.

## THE FLESH CONNECTION

It is difficult to disagree with the contention that in contemporary America, the emphasis in terms of male and female relationships is strictly on the physical. Two commercials demonstrate this: the Coca Cola commercial of the well-built man who draws a crowd of female office workers as he removes his shirt to drink a Coke; the underwear commercial in which a number of women gaze upon a man walking around in his apartment in his shorts. The emphasis in on the physical. Of course, there is the old familiar habit of men watching women. However, there is a new twist to this age-old girl-watching "male thing"—today's woman is stripped down to her underwear and is shown on mass media in the most seductive setting.

This social focus on the physical has produced a generation of men and women who have little sense of and regard for the individual who lives in the well-defined slim body. Thus, for more than a few relationships the thing that brings the couple together is what is referred to as the "flesh connection."

In the flesh connection, the priority in the relationship is physical attractiveness and sexuality of the individual. In this kind of relationship there is little room for growth and development in terms of courtship with a view to marriage. This is the kind of relationship that moves swiftly to sexual involvement. Single men and women are often unaware of the risk involved in being physically attractive. Physically attractive men or women do well to be aware of the fact that they are prime targets for flesh connection relationships.

Mary was a beautiful child and very smart. Her mother and father divorced when she was a small child so she and her siblings grew up in a single parent home. In addition to being a beautiful child, Mary was also intelligent. She was an "A" student in school. When Mary finished high school her mother sent her off to college with enough scholarship money to pay her way through school. With sufficient money and a natural ability to learn fast, it was a foregone conclusion that she would achieve her goal in life and become a professional woman in the field of her choice. However, Mary's mother did not realize at the time, the high visibility Mary's beauty would give her in college. In short order, Mary was faced with the challenge of focusing on her studies at college or responding to the many young men who were pursuing her because of her beauty.

Mary like many young men and women was unprepared to manage her beauty in the context of college; she became involved in a variety of flesh connection relationships and flunked out of college. Beauty and brains are a good combination, but young men and women must be prepared emotionally to manage their physical attractiveness in such a way that it does not abort their path to success.

One of the long standing stereotypes of African-American men is that they are much better at initiating relationships than developing and maintaining them. As an African-American man and pastor who has ministered to thousands of African-American men and women over a period of more than three decades, I am inclined to agree that in many instances such is the case.

I am not arguing that Anglo men are better at developing and maintaining relationships with women than are African-American men. I am merely focusing on the men to whom I minister. The African-American male demonstrates an ability to talk with almost any woman which enables him to initiate a relationship with the woman. However, that same man will most often struggle to develop and maintain that relationship for a long period of time. The results of this is that the African-American male is often involved in several flesh connection relationships simultaneously. Relationships initiated in this context are for the most part flesh connection relationships with little hope of surviving in the context of time and circumstances.

The beauty of the African-American woman is well-documented and has been for many years. Likewise, the handsomeness of the African-American man is known. This natural physical attractiveness is often the primary thing that brings together these men and women in dating and courtship. However, this flesh connection must never be viewed as anything more than the stuff of which lust is made. Genuine relationships must ultimately have a heart connection.

## THE CASH CONNECTION

The cash connection differs from the flesh connection in a number of ways depending upon the age and gender involved. This connection consists of a relationship in which the attraction is money and what it can provide. It has little regard for the individual apart from the money. Men and women who choose to involve themselves in a cash connection relationship must know that they are setting themselves up for hurt in heartless relationships.

The cash connection is not about beauty or handsomeness, nor is it about the ability of men to converse well with women. The cash connection is about material things that gratify the flesh. It is about immediate tangible self-gratification. There are two groups of people who are highly susceptible to cash connection type relationships: the young African-American female with an older man and the young African-American male with an older female.

## A BIBLICAL EXAMPLE

Second Samuel 13 records the experience of a young woman and man who got caught in the unforgiving net of the flesh and cash connection. The story in this chapter is about the young and beautiful woman Tamar and the young and handsome man, Amnon. The beauty of Tamar was such that it attracted the attention of Amnon to the point that he was depressed because he could not have her.

It is important to note that the text says that Amnon loved Tamar. However, this love that Amnon felt for Tamar was strictly lust. In other words, it was a flesh connection, having nothing at all to do with Tamar as a person. I have often heard young men say to young women that they love them so much that it hurts. I do not doubt that when such things are said the young man actually means it. They are in reality expressing the desire of their libido.

Tamar was a young woman with a multitude of quality characteristics and abilities. Her potential for developing into a professional woman with the option to marry and become a mother was as great as was any other young woman of her day. She was not a flirt and was not acting in a seductive manner. In fact, Tamar was an innocent young woman inclined to trust herself in situations.

Amnon on the other hand was a young man from an upper class family. His father was the king. One could assume that he was cultured and educated in the manner that the sons of kings were. Yet in this situation his attitude and behavior were driven by his libido, not by his status.

The beauty of Tamar caught the eye of Amnon and he wanted to be with her so badly that his inability to figure out a way to have her caused him to become depressed to the point that he became dysfunctional. The evident depression of Amnon caught the eye of his friend, Jonadab, who was the son of Amnon's father's brother. This friend was also Amnon's cousin and was noted for his craftiness. This cunning friend worked out a scheme for Amnon to get what he wanted from Tamar.  The fact that Amnon's friend had to devise a scheme for him might suggest that Amnon was not a shrewd schemer—just a good boy in heat.

Amnon, like most young single men and women, needed a friend to teach him how to manage his desires. This friend, however, taught him how to exploit others and fulfill his selfish desires. Amnon had his own apartment and servants in accordance with the lifestyle of the son of the king. The plan was to find a way to get Tamar to his apartment alone with him and then get her into his bedroom and ultimately into his bed. In

many ways Amnon was not unlike many middle class
African-American young men who have all of the trap-
pings of their economic status and nothing to do with
their time and energy. Such young men are prime
prospects for flesh and cash connection relationships.
Without recounting the scheme, let me simply say
that it was rooted in deception driven by lust without
regard for the future of the beautiful young woman.
The scheme was suited to Amnon's lifestyle—a young
man with money and power at his disposal.

Consider the change in Amnon's attitude and behavior towards Tamar immediately after he satisfied his
lust. Before Amnon fulfilled his lust by raping Tamar,
he felt that he was desperately in love with her to the
point of frustration and depression. After his lust was
sated, he threw her out. What before had felt life love
turned into a feeling of hate and disgust.

It is interesting to note that lust unfulfilled has no
regard for morality. Satisfied lust has no regard or respect for the person or their beauty. Lust has no regard
for the individual and is concerned only with satisfying
itself. Once that is done the person is tossed aside like a
used paper towel. Love on the other hand is concerned
about the individual and will do what is necessary to
protect the individual. Love has the quality of patience
and time is love's best friend. Thus the difference between lust and love.

When one profiles lust, it looks like the focus is entirely on the physical. It is pregnant with sin and when
it is finished, it brings forth death. Such was the case
with Amnon. He loved Tamar's body and lusted after it.
He did not want to be committed to her as a husband
nor was he prepared to take the time to build a relationship with her. He wanted her immediately. To get what
he wanted from Tamar, Amnon disregarded all spiritual principles of honesty and integrity. Lust has no regard for right and wrong and is totally devoid of any integrity. Once satisfied, lust turned to hatred towards its
object and threw her away to bear her shame. Considering how both of their lives turned out after this event,

Amnon's sin essentially ended both their lives. Sin, when it is finished, brings forth death.

My files are filled with Tamars who had their encounter with an Amnon and were left to live their lives as best they could having been robbed of their innocence because they were beautiful. In this story, Amnon's lust caused him to rape Tamar and thereby ruin both their lives. In contemporary settings lust may take the wing of consentual sex, date rape, or incest. The results are often the same—shattered lives.

I was shopping in a store some time ago and came to the checkout counter. As I stood there waiting, I noticed that the checker was a beautiful young African-American woman about twenty years old. Standing a few feet from her was a young African-American man about thirty years old. What caught my attention was the obvious line this man was "laying" on this beautiful young girl. The man was so good that I noticed that the young woman was about to be persuaded and go out with this young man.

When I got to the counter I said to the young woman, "He wants you to go out with him doesn't he?" "Yes sir," she replied. "Will you?" I inquired. "I am not sure" she responded. I said to the young woman "You know he only wants your body because you are beautiful, don't you?" I suggested to this young woman that she disregard this man because it was most likely only his lust that motivated him, not her as a person. Having said that I went on my way hoping I had given this young woman something to think about.

# CHAPTER 8

# SINGLENESS AND CELIBACY: A BIBLICAL DISTINCTION

Singleness is a state of being in which a person, for some reason, is not married or no longer married. The gift of celibacy, on the other hand, is a chosen lifestyle in which the Christian chooses not to marry and thus denies himself or herself the pleasures of sex and reproduction for the sake of God's call to vocational Christian service. Celibacy requires of the person who chooses it that this person have the gift of self-control. It is possible, however, for a person to be single and not sexually active and have celibacy as their moral practice and not have the gift of self-control and not be in possession of the gift of celibacy. Marriage is the more attractive option for this person.

It is assumed by most Christians that to be single is to have the gift of celibacy. In the minds of those who think this way, being single and being morally pure means that such a person is in possession of the gift of celibacy. There is a difference in the practice of celibacy which is abstention from sex outside of marriage and the gift of celibacy. From a biblical perspective celibacy is a spiritual choice not a result of the social context in which more than a few African-American women live because there is a scarcity of available men to marry. This choice must be accompanied by the gift of self-control. Abstaining from sexual immorality is not the same as the choice of celibacy which is accompanied by the gift of self-control. Sexual purity is the way of sanctification for *all* Christians; celibacy is the spiritual choice of some Christian men and women.

As a seminary professor who has served as associate dean of students for a number of years, I have observed a number of single men and women who have come to seminary having sensed the call of God in their lives to enter into full-time vocational Christian service. These single adults are committed to moral purity and thus practice celibacy in their relationships. However, only those who have the gift of celibacy will forego the option to marry in deference to the call of God into vocational Christian service. For those who do not have the gift of celibacy, the absence of a mate creates a void in their lives. For those who have the gift of celibacy, the ministry completely fills that void.

For the Christian who is single for any reason other than a choice based on a spiritual calling and is without the gift of self-control, abstaining from sex is a major consistent struggle. 1 Corinthians 7:9 says that the single person who does not have self-control should marry, for it is better to marry than to burn in lustful passion. The idea here is that the person who does not have the gift of self-control will in spite of his singleness feel compelled to fully express his sexual urges; however, because he is single and saved, being sexually active is not an option for him. Thus, it is highly possible that such a single will spend much of his/her time craving sexual companionship. This feeling of compulsion is what it means to burn in one's sexual passion. This persistent struggle often causes the single adult to be vulnerable to shallow relationships and emotional exploitation. I have found this to be especially true of the Christian African-American female. Persistent burning in one's sexual desires can also lead to homosexual activity (Rom. 1:27).

In such cases where this kind of struggle is occurring and there is no discipleship and personal accountability, the Christian single can hardly be expected to grow spiritually. His/her mind is filled with lustful, sexual thoughts.

As I have pointed out, the social context in which the African-American female finds herself today is one in which there is a shortage of available African-American men for marriage. Thus, many African-American females must face the reality of not having marriage to an African-American male as a viable option. In the context of the gift of celibacy and the practice of celibacy, one has to consider the fact that there are several different kinds of single people in terms of why they're single. There are the unwed single parents who have children out of wedlock, often at an early age; singles who are divorced and single adults who are widowed. The largest group of singles in the African-American community is single females who have never married.

## THE SOCIAL CONTEXT

In the context of those who have not married as well as those who have married and are single again for whatever reason, the issue of celibacy is a very real question that must be faced on a daily basis. It is the responsibility of all Christian singles to practice celibacy by abstaining from sexual immorality, but the gift of celibacy is most likely not something singles who have been previously married can expect to have. Only in rare instances, have I seen cases in which a single person seemed to have been given the gift of celibacy after having been married.

Then there are Christian singles who have chosen to forego the option to marry, choosing rather to give themselves fully to the ministry. These people have the gift of self-control and find strength to resist the tendency to burn in their sexual passion.

## THE RIGHT TO CHOOSE

It is the custom in our culture to allow people who desire to be married to choose mates for themselves. The clear assumption inherent in this practice is that every man has the option to choose a mate and every woman will be chosen by a man.

This is a false assumption of major proportion in our day. There are men who never feel they have the option to choose and some women who are never chosen. In such cases, the single state in which these Christians find themselves does not mean that they have the gift of celibacy, but they do practice celibacy. Celibacy has really nothing to do with the opportunity for marriage or the lack. It is rooted in the Christian's spiritual choice in opting for Christian service regardless of opportunity or lack of opportunity for marriage.

When a virgin Christian, for whatever the reason, does not attract a mate and begins to get beyond the marrying age (in view of the danger of a lack of self-control as it pertains to sex), it may be that the parents should take the responsibility of arranging a marriage for that son or daughter (1 Cor. 7:36). However, for parents who do not feel compelled to arrange a marriage for their child, choosing rather to allow them to remain single may be a better option. This is because marriage carries with it certain demands that must be met sometimes at great sacrifice.

## MORE PROBLEMS THAN ANSWERS

In my experience as a pastor in the African-American community, I have seen some cases in which it seemed as if the Christian couple was marrying in order to have access to what I refer to as "sanctified sex" as opposed to a holistic need-based relationship. I refer to these kinds of relationships as "jockey shorts" or "Calvin Klein" relationships. In these instances, a Christian single man and woman come together in their passion for the physical rather than coming together with a holistic recognized need for each other.

These kinds of relationships, once consummated, are often filled with problems because the compelling force that brought them together is the "flesh connection" as opposed to the "heart connection." Therefore, it is critical that single Christians understand the need to manage their bodies and all of their desires in such a way that they glorify God. The single Christian must set high moral standards for themselves with a priority on personal sanctification. These high moral standards must include the will to live sacrificially.

The single Christian must develop personal discipline in their emotional and moral life which will produce stability and consistency in their walk with God. This means learning to delay sexual gratification until such time that one is able to enter into the kind of relationship that leads to companionship in the context of marriage. The alternative to developing discipline is allowing ones self to become a person who is fragmented in the sharing of themselves.

## You Can Trust God

Being open to God's timing in terms of when, as well as who to date, court and marry is of utmost importance for the single Christian. God may not provide a mate when your friends are getting married and you are getting older. Instead, He may be calling you to a ministry which necessitates you being single. The single Christian must discard the idea that marriage must take place sooner in life, rather than later in life. You can trust God to lead you and guide you in this area. If it is His will that you marry, He will be faithful in directing, whether it be sooner or later.

Single Christians must accent the spiritual in terms of who it is that they court with the potential of marrying. I am of the opinion that all courtship should have marriage as its goal. There is a difference between courtship and dating. This means being willing to date and court with a view to marrying the person God brings into your life, even though that person might not meet all of your ideal physical expectations.

CHAPTER 9

# THE SINGLE PARENT AND THE PARENTING PROCESS

I have sought to establish the idea that in order to have a positive attitude toward being single, this state for the adult male and female is best perceived as a matter of choice, rather than social, domestic, or economic compulsion.

The single parent brings to that most important process of parenting some serious challenges that must be considered in order to avoid the possibility of parenting ending in defeat. These problems include unfulfilled, persistent sexual passions that are intensified by the reality of past sexual experiences. These past experiences cause the single parent to experience loneliness at a level that can be very unsettling. The fact that a single person is a parent is evidence that he does not have the gift of celibacy or did not choose it as a way of life.

## THE CHALLENGES OF THE SINGLE PARENT

As it pertains to parenting, the single parent faces the same long challenging process of growing an adult as does the married parent. Both the married parent and the single parent are beset with certain inherent deficiencies in the parenting process which are very similar. However, the single parent must understand that attempts at fulfilling the felt need for sexual expression and persistent loneliness will cost much in terms of the child's or children's respect for them as a parent.

Usually children are ill-equipped to deal with the idea of their parent courting. In our culture, courting is perceived to be the domain of the young and single non-parent. The challenge of the Christian single parent, therefore, is to consider the possibility of foregoing the fulfillment of sexual desires in the context of marriage and living with the emotional struggles of persistent loneliness until the child or children are emotionally prepared to handle the courtship and marriage of their parent. In reality, this may mean that a parent must choose between an active sex life in the context of marriage and that of remaining a single parent without such a relationship. In many instances, the child or children will not accept a step-parent without serious rebellion.

## THE TRAGEDY OF OUR TIMES

Single parenting is the fastest growing method of raising children in the African-American community today. Close to 51 percent of all African-American children are born outside of marriage. This means that there are several different categories of single parents in our community today. They are the unwed mothers and fathers who have never married. A large number of these are teenage boys and girls. We have divorced parents or those parents who are separated but not divorced. We also have the widowed parent. Finally, there are single parents who adopt.

The age category of single parents is as low as twelve years old. But, whatever the age, being a single parent is a major challenge.

Single parenting is not God's ideal context for raising children into healthy adults. In addition, single parents usually face pressing economic problems. The largest number of poor in America today are the children of single parents. The African-American community has a disproportionate number of these poor children. The challenge to the single parent, most of whom are women, is providing money, education, food, shelter and clothing. This challenge can be overwhelming. No wonder the largest number of people living in poverty today are children of single parents. These are women who for the most part are overwhelmed by the impossible odds of providing holistically for their children in urban and rural America. Furthermore, social problems such as loneliness often plague the single parent to a far greater degree than the single person who has no children. For single parents, domestic limitations usually mean their mobility is limited. In addition, the limitations of only one gender in the home to model the nuclear family ideal cause a serious imbalance. There is also the problem of how to exercise discipline and respect for authority in positive relationships.

Single parents generally produce children who themselves become single parents. Single parent households often raise children with low self-esteem. Sometimes there are feelings of insecurity because all too often, children of single parents grow up in poverty in many rural communities, but especially in the large inner cities of our country. All too often these children are the ones joining gangs because of not having a positive two-parent family model.

While being a single parent is not God's ideal for growing children into healthy adults, success is not impossible. Single parents, most of whom are women, must rest in the sovereign power of the living God to direct them in the parenting process. This means being willing to make the kind of hard decisions about their social lives in deference to what is best for the child or children. It means being a woman of prayer with personal spiritual accountability.

The disproportionate number of single African-American mother in this country is really not the fault of the African-American woman. The flip side of single African-American mothers is the unemployed and under employed African-American male. The 1989 United States Senate Select Committee hearing on the vanishing African-American male established the fact that the employed African-American male demonstrates the same kind of commitment to his family as does any other father in America. The unemployed father demonstrates just the opposite.

In considering the positive impact a good mother can have on her children, consider Jochebed, the mother of Moses. All the major players in the early life of Moses were women. They included the midwives, Moses' mother, his sister and the daughter of the Pharaoh. In the first three years of Moses' life, his mother shaped his character so that thirty-seven years of Egyptian education and culture could not wipe it out.

I say that Moses' mother was in partnership with God in the parenting process. She and God raised a leader who changed the fate of His people. It is this kind of mothering that the single mother must do if she is to be successful in spite of the challenges.

# CHAPTER 10

# SINGLENESS AND CHRISTIAN SERVICE

For a Christian adult, singleness at its best must be a choice rather than a social consequence in order to be perceived as a positive social state in which to be. That person who is not single by choice will most often feel deprived. Thus, the positive-minded single person must answer the question for herself—"Would I marry if I could?" Only when the answer is "No! because . . ." is there the possibility of a positive attitude toward the single life. The *because* can be the call of God to a ministry that is best done without the distraction of a mate. Too often a married person is distracted from the ministry by the responsibility of pleasing his or her mate.

The decision not to marry may also be due to the death of one's mate which cannot be filled by anyone else. Marriage is a serious step and each person has the privilege of deciding whether or not his/her particular circumstances make it desirable or practical.

## COMMITTED TO SERVE

While it is true that every Christian has the responsibility of being seriously involved in the ministry in obedience to the great commission, some Christians are called to a vocation of ministry. For the vocational Christian worker, the context may be such that a person who is not married would be the better option. For example, the single minister may be able to live at a higher risk as it pertains to economic stability and social environment. In addition, the single minister has a single focus in terms of relationships that centers on pleasing the Lord alone.

In 1 Corinthians 7, the apostle Paul makes the argument that both the married and single states are positive positions for ministry. However, he goes on to point out that there are times in which the environment in which one is called to minister is such that God calls one to a life of celibacy which is accompanied by the gift of self-control.

In this text of 1 Corinthians 7, both marriage and celibacy are gifts and callings from God. Thus, in terms of maximizing one's singleness, it is imperative that all Christian singles determine for themselves that to which God has called them in terms of Christian service. This will help determine whether they should marry or not and when.

There is the appeal from God in Romans 12:1-2 to all believers to give themselves to the Lord as a living sacrifice, which is their reasonable service of worship. They are not to conform to this world, choosing rather to be transformed by being renewed in their minds in order that they might know what the will of God is for their lives. These two verses say to the Christian single that the first order of business is in his/her spiritual walk is to get their life on track. This is done by responding to the grace and mercy of God, which has been so generously bestowed and by giving your body to the Lord as an act of worship to Him. This means that the single person will no longer lay claim to his body as being his own.

## MANAGING LONELINESS AS A SINGLE ADULT

For those saints who are abstaining and have the gift of celibacy, loneliness usually is not a major issue; for they find their total fulfillment in their service to the Lord. This is not to say that they do not enjoy the company of the opposite sex. It is to say, however, that they do not struggle with feelings of loneliness. They can accept their loneliness as a consequence of their spiritual vocational choice.

The focus of this study, however, is on that single adult who is not married and yet feels the need for somebody with whom to share themselves. In other words, they want to be married. In this context, loneliness is a deep, persistent, emotional response to the absence of somebody of the opposite sex with whom to share one's whole person. Loneliness in this context is the adult emotional feeling that results from the absence of companionship with the opposite sex.

## BEING ALONE VERSUS BEING LONELY

It is important to distinguish between what it means to feel alone and what it means to feel lonely. The person who feels alone may be experiencing a psychological reaction to being excluded from a conversation, a game or a party. To feel alone is to feel temporarily left out of something; it is possible to be in a crowd and feel alone. On the other hand, loneliness is something more than feeling temporarily left out of something. Loneliness is an emotional response to the absence of a companion with whom to share one's total person on an on-going basis.

It is good to recall for a moment Genesis 2:18, in which God said of the man Adam that is was not good for him to be alone. Thus, he made for Adam a woman who corresponded to him to be his helper. I take it that what is in view here is a word from God about how a man is designed. The point being that man is above all else a social creature and is therefore in need of somebody who corresponds to what he is; but who is not biologically, physiologically, or emotionally identical to himself with whom to share his complete person. God created Eve as just such a person for Adam.

On the other hand, it is to be noted that the woman Eve was never alone from the moment of her creation; she was joined to the man Adam. I take it that, above all else, women have a social need to feel needed by and to belong to a man. For Eve, Adam was that somebody to whom she felt needed and to whom she belonged. Thus, we have two social beings, a man who needs a companion and a woman who needs to be needed as a companion. The solution is marriage.

There are three dimensions to men and women that fit this companionship-loneliness context: the physical, the emotional, and the spiritual.

## The Physical

The first step towards managing loneliness is understanding that this feeling is the body's way of signaling the arrival of full-blown adulthood. Full-blown adulthood means maturity at the level of the heart, mind and body. Let me point out that there is a difference between loneliness and awakening of sexual urges in the maturing young boy or girl. The latter is basically hormonal and is related to the libido and rooted primarily in the physical. Loneliness, on the other hand, is rooted in the arrival of emotional, spiritual, and physical adulthood. It is a signal of the need for a companion with whom to share one's whole person. Thus, the arrival of loneliness is the body and spirit's way of declaring that the cycle of maturity has been completed and the individual is now prepared for the responsibilities of adulthood in the context of a marriage relationship. The person who is unable or unwilling to enter into the process of courtship that leads to the fulfillment of the need for companionship will experience loneliness.

## The Emotional

Secondly, managing loneliness means developing personal discipline in the area of emotional and moral stability. This means learning to delay such things as sexual gratification until one is able to enter into the formal relationship that leads to companionship. The alternative to developing discipline is allowing oneself to become a person who is fragmented in the sharing of themselves. In such a situation, the person may be involved in several different relationships from which they extract something that they may want for themselves at the moment, but they never move into a companionship relationship.

*The Spiritual*

Finally, managing loneliness means being open to God's timing in terms of when and who to marry. This means coming to grips with the fact that God may not provide a mate based on your timetable, but only on His own. To this end, one must discard the common misconception that marriage must take place sometimes before age thirty. Managing loneliness means being willing to consider, in a serious way, the person that God brings into your life as a potential companion even though he or she might not meet all of your ideal physical expectations. The timing is in God's hands, as well as the choice, if you really desire God's will for your life.

## CONCLUSION

The single woman and the single man both have what I call "high archways of needs." For the woman, these needs include the need to feel protected, the need to feel secure, and the need for a positive intimate relationship. In all too many instances, the single woman looks exclusively to a man to meet these needs. The problem is that for more than a few African-American women, there are too few men available to respond to such needs. Surely the Christian African-American woman cannot even consider the idea of sharing some other woman's mate, as is advocated by some nationalistic-minded African-American sociologists today. The underlying idea of such a degrading suggestion is that this is the tradition of African communities from which the African-American was extracted.

As Christians, the African-American female must look to God as the source from which she is to get her needs met. In response to her felt need for protection, God the Father is the ultimate protector (Ps. 23). Her need for shepherding is met through the Good Shepherd, God's Son (John 10). The single woman's need for affirmation is found in God the Holy Spirit, the ultimate comforter (John 16).

The single Christian woman must not consider her singleness as a social deprivation. Rather she must view singleness as spiritual exaltation in that all she needs she gets directly from God without the distraction of having to please a husband.

The African-American male also has a high-archway of needs that include the need to shepherd, the need to provide, the need to initiate. These needs for the African-American male are traditionally met in his marriage. However, the single Christian male must find expression and fulfillment of these needs in his relationship with God. The indwelling Spirit of God through the single man can develop a ministry through which he can shepherd, provide, and affirm. The idea that every man must be married to have an effective ministry is not so. The fact is that through the local church, at home and abroad, the single man can fully express himself and find fulfillment of his needs.

## So What?

If we are to believe the message of seduction and sex constantly flashed before us in the media, then there is no way to enjoy the single life apart from living in raw moral sin. Fun means freedom without responsibility. Fun means immorality without consequences. There is ample evidence that such a lifestyle is not all that it is cracked up to be.

For every single Christian there is a choice and a challenge. The choice is deciding to go against the tide of the moral climate of our time and embrace moral purity to the glory of God. The challenge is to take advantage of every opportunity to shine as God's light in the context in which one lives.

# CHAPTER 11

# THE CHRISTIAN WOMAN

For some single women the idea of being single for the rest of their lives is something less than exciting. I have often found that single women who desire to be married and are not moving towards that goal have something less than a strong hope that the Lord will indeed provide a husband for them.

This chapter is for single women. The principles are taken from the story of Ruth who was widowed at an early age and yet did not lose hope. She chose rather to glean in hope in the field of the sovereignty of God.

## A BRIEF SUMMARY

In chapter one of the Book of Ruth, the primary focus is on Naomi. Naomi was a clear picture of a woman who found herself living on the downside of the sovereignty of God. Naomi teaches us that life on the downside of God's sovereignty can lead to carnal choices with dire consequences. So many Christians are caught in the throes of trying to find for themselves a better life and in the process do as Naomi and her husband did. They moved beyond the boundaries of the people of God.

In this age of prosperity, there are times when it is the will of God that His people have less not more. In these times Christians sometimes make carnal choices in their attempt to escape the will of God by moving away from their spiritual commitment into a more worldly context. Such was the case with Naomi.

## PRINCIPLES FROM RUTH

Ruth came to Bethlehem from Moab with her former mother-in-law where they both had been devastated by their life experiences. She was a young, single woman—a minority in a foreign land. Ruth turned her attention to what I call "Gleaning in hope in the field of the sovereignty of God."

So devastating was life in Moab for Naomi that she changed her name from Naomi which meant "pleasant" to Mara which meant "bitter." This change was Naomi's way of proclaiming that the Almighty had witnessed against her. She left home full; God had brought her home empty. I take it that Naomi's life experience was reflective of carnal choices and the price tag for those choices was costly.

Out of this social, economic, and domestic devastation emerged a spirit in Ruth that is both interesting and attractive. Ruth developed a desire to go out and glean in the barley fields where the men were and where one man in particular could see her.

As a gleaner Ruth was confined to the portion of the fields that had already been harvested. She was one among many women who was poor and followed after the harvesters collecting grain for bread from what was left behind.

Ruth hoped somebody would be kind enough to let her glean in their field even though she was not of their race or culture. I find this spirit in Ruth to be very attractive because she was a single woman with no visible hope of survival apart from God's sovereign intervention into her circumstances. Ruth ventured out and gleaned in the field of hope in the sovereignty of God.

In the field of God's sovereignty character is important. Ruth was a woman of character. She knew the meaning of commitment. She found herself caught in the nightmare of disaster. She had lost everything of value to her, and was faced with the choice of returning to paganism or following the living God whom she had come to know through her husband. Ruth unlike her sister-in-law, said to Naomi her mother-in-law, "Where you go, I will go, and where you lodge, I will lodge. Your people shall be my people, and your God, my God" (Ruth 1:16).

Ruth was a woman of optimism. She expected the best from God. She said to Naomi, "Please let me go to the field and glean among the ears of grain after one in whose sight I may find favor" (2:2). Ruth had no husband and no relatives anywhere among the nation of Israel where she had chosen to live.

Here is a lesson single women would do well to learn: It is not always your privilege to live in the midst of plenty. Sometimes you may find yourself in a situation in which the resources are scarce. In such situations do not let your circumstances choke out your expectations of God. Ruth believed that even in the field where the crops had already been gathered there was enough grain left to feed Naomi and herself. In tough times keep your focus on God not your circumstances.

When Ruth went out into the field to gather grain for food she was in a real sense seeking God's favor in the field of His sovereignty. As a single woman Ruth teaches this lesson. In the field of the sovereignty of God the scarcity of the desired resource makes no difference as it pertains to God's ability to meet the needs of His people. Single women today need to be reassured of the fact that no matter what scarcities they face (men, job, money, food), God is able to provide.

I find more than a few single women today who seem to have given up hope of ever having their needs met. They seem to have concluded that for them total fulfillment in this life is no longer to be expected. So in a spirit of despair they go from one hopeless and depressing day to the next.

Many a single woman has conceded defeat as it pertains to getting married to a good man. This conclusion is based on their knowledge of the scarcity of African-American men who are available for marriage. Out of this spirit of hopelessness some Christian women marry men who are unsaved; others live in and out of moral sin.

There is something more to be considered in the context of scarcity, namely the sovereignty of God. The issue is not how much is left but rather how one can find favor with God; it is His favor and His favor alone that determines the affairs of the life of His children. Single women must learn to glean in the field of the sovereignty of God.

When Ruth went out to glean in the field she knew nothing of whose field it was but God knew. He guided her to the field of Boaz who was a very wealthy relative of Naomi. In this context I must point out that Boaz's field was God's field and in God's field there is always a spirit of compassion. Ruth found favor with the reapers in the first field at which she stopped, having been led there by the sovereignty of God.

## THE HARVEST OF DIVINE PROVISION

Many single Christians live each day of their lives in the nightmare of the fear of failure. They spend no small amount of time and energy trying to escape even the prospect of failure. The three main things single women fear failing are finances, parenting, and the option to marry. These fears are camouflaged by most single women; nevertheless, they are there.

Naomi and Ruth were two women who were living in failure. Their failure, according to the testimony of Naomi, was the result of the hand of God being against her because of her life choices. When the hand of God is against anybody for any reason they are in trouble. This is no less true in the lives of single Christians who make carnal choices in life. Failure in the lives of many single women is the result of their carnal choices most often made in the context of getting for herself that which is scarce.

Robert Schuller says, "Success is never ending and failure is never final." I say in the sovereignty of God failure does not prohibit God from protecting and providing for His own. When Christians fail, does God still provide for and protect them or is life after failure simply a miserable tumble down hill from then on?

For the answer to this question look at Ruth in the sovereignty of God. God placed in Boaz's mind the idea that he was to use his power and influence to protect and provide for Ruth. Thus, Boaz told Ruth to stay with his harvesters and not to glean in another field because someone might hurt her. He had instructed the servants not to touch her. In this we see how God provided for and protected this single woman who was a minority in a foreign country. Boaz told Ruth to drink from his servant's jar when she was thirsty. Clearly this is evidence of divine provision and protection for a young single woman.

In the midst of the provision and protection Boaz was providing for Ruth, she asked him why he was doing all of this for her. Boaz answer is quite instructive, "All that you have done for your mother-in-law after the death of your husband has been fully reported to me, and how you left your father and your mother and the land of your birth, and came to a people that you did not previously know" (2:11). In the sovereignty of God kind deeds are never wasted. Every kind deed is an investment that pays dividends in this life.

What a significant time in the life of Ruth. The fruit of her kindness to her mother-in-law came to fulfillment. Right in the midst of her failed life, God showed up with the dividends for her kindness to Naomi.

Boaz further said to Ruth, "May the Lord reward your work and your wages be full from the Lord the God of Israel under whose wings you have come to seek refuge" (2:12). In the midst of failure God often looks as it were into the record book of kind deeds done by His children and cashes in the investment and give the dividends to His servant. In the sovereignty of God His provision and protection are tied to our service and commitment to Him.

## HOPE FOR A BETTER DAY

When Ruth went home after a day of gleaning in the field of Boaz she carried with her not only enough grain to feed herself and Naomi, but she also had gained the favor of a wealthy man. In the field of God's sovereignty there is always hope for a better day.

I think sometimes that the reason there is so much discouragement among single women in the church is because they have ceased to glean in this land of scarcity in the field of God's sovereignty. As a result their hope is small and their joy is scarce.

It is only in the field of God's sovereignty that the single woman can find the basis for hope in a hopeless situation. Thus when circumstances are such that they strip you of all hope of a better day choose to take your case to the field of the sovereignty of God and there glean in hope of a better day.

When I say glean in the field of God's sovereignty I do not mean that there is any scarcity in that field for there is always an abundance of grace and mercy in God's field of sovereignty. I am simply making the point to the single African-American woman that when there is a scarcity that is, a good time to go out and glean in God's field. In that field there is just what you need and then some.

# CHAPTER 12

# SINGLE SAINTS

The single African American Christian faces many challenges today that are exciting, challenging, and sometimes intimidating. The church today in many instances seems uncertain about its role in ministering effectively to the single saint. While the church diligently strives to find its way in its ministry to single Christians, it seems that each individual believer must understand the nature of the spiritual struggle that must be faced on a daily basis.

## UNDERSTANDING THE STRUGGLE

In studying the Book of Ephesians, I find it interesting that God's instructions to believers regarding developing and maintaining strong and healthy relationships with each other and the family, is sandwiched between the command to be filled with the Spirit (Eph. 5:18) and the exhortation to stand against the powers of evil (6:10).

I gather from this divine arrangement the idea that every believer must understand and appreciate the value of strong relationships in the church and in the home. To develop and maintain such relationships the Christian must depend on the power of the Holy Spirit in order to develop and maintain a Christian environment in the home. A Christian home is not just for married people. The single Christian is also responsible before God to develop and maintain a Christian environment in their home as are married people. I further conclude from this divine arrangement that the Christian home is the persistent target of the powers of evil.

Christians must understand that the target of the devil and his demons is not the church congregation collectively, but the individual families who make up the membership of the local church. The devil knows that to the extent that he is able to break down and then break up the Christian environment in the home thereby destroying the Christian attitude of family members, he will in time effectively negate the power and influence of the gospel of Jesus Christ.

To understand the nature of the spiritual struggle Christian singles face today, a study of Ephesians 6:10-12 may be helpful. The focus of this section of Ephesians is on finishing well in our walk with and service to the Lord. For the Christian there is nothing left to be won. The battle has already been fought between Jesus and Satan. Jesus won that battle once and for all. The task of the believer is not to win anything; all we must do is stand in the victory that Jesus has already won.

The focus in this text is not on a fight or a battle with the powers of evil, but on a struggle between the believer and the powers of evil. We must therefore understand that the whole of the Christian life is a constant struggle between the believer and the devil with his demons.

There is a difference between the spiritual struggle that we have with the devil and the spiritual fight Jesus had with the devil. In the fight that Jesus had with the devil, the goal was to win or prevail over the devil and all the powers of evil once and for all. In our struggle with the devil, the objective is to stand in the victory Christ won in His fight with the devil. We are to stand in spite of the persistent entanglement of our adversary the devil. Let me reiterate: Jesus and the devil had the spiritual fight. . . . Jesus defeated the devil once and for all. . . . The believer and the devil are in a struggle. . . . Our responsibility is to stand in the victory won by Jesus on Calvary.

In Ephesians 5:18 the command to all believers is to be filled with the Spirit. In this state of being controlled by the Spirit, the believer sings, prays, and submits, one to the other, all in ways that are beyond his or her natural attitude and behavior. The filling of the Spirit is all about worship, praise, service, family, and career. It is about living a supernatural lifestyle in the context of everyday life.

In Ephesians 6:10 the command is be strong in the Lord and in the power of His might. The focus here is on how you finish the Christian life given the inevitable lifetime struggle with Satan and his imps. The major challenges for the single saint are finishing well in life and service to the Lord.

The difference between the filling for the living and the strengthening for the standing is the difference between the power and influence of the flesh (Rom. 7; Gal. 5), and the power and influence of Satan and his imps (Eph. 6:10ff). In the former, the struggle is with ones own internal depravity; with the latter the struggle is with the external forces of evil that are headed by Satan himself. With the former, the believer's victory is based on his/her willingness to yield to the power of the Holy Spirit. With the latter, believer's victory is based on his/her willingness to do all that is necessary to stand . . . having been dressed themselves in the full armor of God.

Ephesians 6:10 says, "Finally, be strong in the Lord and in the strength of His might." The text could read: Be fortified with power. Compare: Ephesians 3:16, "that He would grant you, according to the riches of His glory, to be strengthened with power through His Spirit in the inner man"; and Colossians 1:11: "strengthened with all power, according to His glorious might for there attaining of all steadfastness and patience." I take it that these verses are saying that the position one must be in to access the power to stand against the devil is in the Lord. The source of the power with which the believer is to be equipped to stand in his/her struggle with the devil is a power that comes from outside. The source of that power is: "strength of His [God's] might." In the context of our constant struggle with the devil, the power that is necessary to finish well in life and service to our Lord in not a strength that can come from an increase which flows from our internal resources.

The single saint who finishes well in life and service to the Lord is the believer who lives the truth expressed in Philippians 4:13, "I can do all things through Him who strengthens me"; "My grace is sufficient for you, for power is perfected in weaknesses; most gladly therefore I would rather boast about my weaknesses, that the power of Christ may dwell in me" (2 Cor. 12:9). Single Christians must refuse to embrace the notion that they can make it in life by drawing upon their own natural strength. They should choose rather to acknowledge their weaknesses along with their struggles.

This strength is "in the Lord." It is the "strength of His power." It must be acknowledged that these words have an implied psychological appeal to the human will and calls saved men and women to a sense of personal courage and determination to finish well in their walk with God. It must be noted, however, that the words of the text are "in the Lord and in His strength."

To say that the believer's strength is in the Lord is to say that those who finish well in their service to the Lord must have a strength that is stronger than self discipline. For this struggle is not about a victory to be won but about a peace to be gained and maintained in the context of our everyday life circumstances, in spite of the opposition of our adversary the devil.

Having alerted believers to the need for the supernatural strength of the living God to stand in their struggle with evil, the text goes on to inform believers that they are not naturally equipped for this struggle. "Put on the full armor of God that you may be able to stand against the schemes of the devil." I take it that the text is saying that the strength believers must have in order to stand in the struggle with the devil is God's strength. We must also note well that the armor that believers must dress themselves in is also God's.

The text says that the substance of the armor in which believers must dress is such that it will be possible to stand and withstand all of the schemes of the devil. You see in order for the armor to protect the saint it must be durable enough to stand up in the struggle no matter how rough the struggle gets. The focus is not on the power that Satan uses to entangle and attempt to put down the believer. No, the focus is on the schemes of the devil. I take it therefore that the emphasis here is on the fact that the powers of the devil and his imps are in the schemes they use to cast down the believer.

When I think of the emphasis God places on the need for both divine power and armor in order to stand against the schemes of the devil, I am compelled to conclude that the devil and his imps are master thinkers and strategists. Numerous and varied are their schemes that are designed to defeat the child of God. Thus, the child of God must be equipped to distinguish between that which seems to be important but is not and that which seems to be unimportant and really is important.

You see Christians, we are no match for the devil at any level. His mind and his experience in defeating and destroying believers are far beyond anything we could possibly survive on our own.

I am a lover of nature. I spend a good deal of time watching films featuring different animals in the wild. I have noticed that when a ravenous lion goes hunting, the survival rate of the prey is solely determined by the decision of the targeted animal to remain with or leave its group. The animal that for whatever reason is cut off from the group becomes a meal for the predator. So it is with single Christians. The devil sets his mind on separating individual single saints from the church or group of believers. Once that is accomplished, the believer will most likely fail.

Our struggle is indeed not with flesh and blood. In order to succeed in this spiritual struggle and thus finish well it is necessary to have a clear understanding of who the enemy is. The enemy of the believer is not other believers, nor is it specifically unsaved people. The struggle is not with flesh and blood.

Some single women think that all men are dogs and must be treated as such. Others tend to think that all a Black man wants from a woman is sex. Some Black men think all women want is someone to take care of them. Then there are those single men and women who have bought into the idea that the White man is the great Satan. The nature of the Christian's spiritual struggle is such that it cannot be with flesh and blood, no matter the race, culture or gender.

The meaning of struggle in Ephesians includes much more than the idea contained in the statement "life is a struggle." In this context its intention is to depict hand-to-hand combat in which the enemy will do and use whatever possible to bring down its opponent. Thus, we must understand as Christians that every day we are in a life and death spiritual struggle with the devil. His single goal is to destroy the child of God by any means necessary.

This life and death struggle is not with people, according to the text. This does not mean that the devil does not use people to carry out his schemes. He has no body through which to work in this world; therefore, he utilizes the minds of people. The devil and his demons must use the mouths of people to spew forth their utterances. These evil spirits must employ the legs and bodies of individuals to infiltrate this or that group of believers for the purpose of destroying their unity and testimonies.

The text is saying that Satan uses people to carry forth his schemes. The believer must understand that the person who has evil on his/her agenda is nothing more than a pawn in the hand of Satan and his imps.

In the recent war between Iraq and Kuwait, President George Bush named it "desert storm" when America got involved. In that war, Iraq's conflict turned out not to be a struggle with Kuwait but with the world's greatest super power—the United States. Had it been a struggle just with Kuwait, Iraq would have easily won the war. Iraq was, however, no match for America. So it is with believers. If our struggles were just with people who hassle or hurt us, no doubt we could easily win most of those battles. However, when it turns out that our struggle is with the world's second supernatural power it quickly becomes evident that we are no match for such a power.

To be in a struggle with the devil in this day means to be in a struggle with any and every individual, idea, value system and standard that represents the devil and his imps. When a country with whom America is at war captures one of its soldiers, that country treats the captive (though it has no particular hate for that individual) as if his/her is America. The reason this is done is because the country knows full well that the loyalty of that captured soldier is with the country to whom he/she belongs. Thus given a chance that hostage will destroy his captors. So it is with the child of God. We must understand that the loyalty of the unsaved is with his master, the devil. Given the opportunity that person (though in a relationship with a child of God) will bring down the Christian's testimony. Single saints must guard themselves against becoming involved with Satan's pawns.

Our struggle is not with flesh and blood but against the rulers, against the powers, against the world forces of this darkness, against the spiritual wickedness in the heavenly places. The rulers, the powers, the worlds forces of darkness and the spiritual wickedness in the heavenly places all refer to the kingdom of Satan. In his kingdom there are myriads of demons of different ranks. There are myriads of ideas, standards and principles that are fitted for doing evil. There are spiritual forces that dominate the atmosphere.

Look again at the words used to describe that which the believer must struggle against and prevail in order to finish well in their life and ministry, rulers, powers, world forces, spiritual wickedness. Ephesians 6:11b exhorts us to stand against the schemes of the devil. I take it that Satan schemes against believers are wrapped in this variety of power packages, thrown into the arena and world of the believer and the death struggle is on.

Now the armor of God is the only equipment that is adequate for such a struggle. Therefore, the believer must put it on to survive the struggle. Again the text in verse 13 says, "Therefore take up the full armor of God" [The purpose] . . . "that you may be able to resist in the evil day" [Results] . . . "having done everything to stand firm."

In conclusion, there is the need in the life of every believer to be equipped with God's power and dressed in God's full armor. The reason believers need such armor is because of who the enemy is. Our struggle is not with flesh and blood.

## GETTING FITTED FOR THE STRUGGLE

I did not play football or any other major sport as a young man growing up in the small town of Lake Providence, Louisiana. Today as an older man, I am not one who attends many sports activities, although I do watch a good deal of football on television from time to time. Now that I have disqualified myself as one who is qualified to speak authoritatively about football, let me speak for a moment about playing the game of football.

To play the game of football, each player must prepare and dress for the particular position he is playing. Since every football team has both offensive and defensive players, some players prepare mentally and dress to some extent to defend the football by attacking the opposing team. Other players are mentally prepared and dress to some degree, to run the ball with a view to scoring against the opposing team.

In football, the defensive team is not responsible for making scores, though they may occasionally do so; the offensive players do that. The offensive team members are not responsible for preventing the opposing team from scoring, though they may occasionally do so; the defensive team does that. The team that finishes well, by successfully standing and withstanding against the strategies of the opposing team, usually wins the game. Such is the case with football.

In the game of life for the Christian about which I know a great deal, the opposing team is the devil and his demons. Every believer is a player in this game. As a player it is the responsibility of every believer to play both the offensive and the defensive side of the spiritual life. This means being mentally prepared and spiritually equipped for both offensive and defensive moves. The armor that God has provided for the Christian in this life struggle is suited just for such a conflict.

Verse 13 says, "Therefore take up the full armor of God" [The purpose] . . . "that you may be able to resist in the evil day" [Results] . . . "having done everything to stand firm." I understand that the text is saying that in light of the nature of the Christian's struggle with the supernatural powers of evil, every Christian must be motivated to put forth the effort to take up and put on God's holy armor. Let me put it this way: Having been informed as to who the opposition is in the Christian life—not flesh and blood, but the devil and his demons, and being enlightened, as to the nature of the struggle, which is against the schemes of the devil, Christians must equip themselves with combat armor. This armor belongs to God and thus is supernatural in substance.

The objective of this armor is for the express purpose of enabling the believer to resist the schemes of the devil in this evil day. In the context of this evil day, every believer must make every effort to accomplish all that is necessary to stand firm. This means that in the Christian's struggle, there is no room for failure. The total objective is to stand and not give an inch.

Before we look at the first three pieces of the armor that the believer is to put on in preparation for standing against the schemes of the devil, let us remind ourselves at this point, that the struggle is against the schemes of the devil. That with which the believer must struggle, and stand, in order to finish well in life and ministry are: rulers, powers, world forces and spiritual wickedness. Verse 11b tells us to stand against the schemes of the devil. I take it that Satan's schemes against believers are wrapped in these different power packages and thrown into the arena and world of the believer and the death struggle is on.

As a single adult it is important to realize that all the forces of hell are aligned against you with one objective; namely, that you not finish well in you life and service to the Lord. This evil against which you must stand as a single saint is not a mere idea, principle, philosophy or standard. No this evil is headed by a real supernatural person, namely Satan.

The first three pieces of armor are truth, righteousness and the gospel of peace. These three pieces of the believer's armor are all virtues of the character of believers. Since each believer must individually put on each piece of this armor, I take it that even though these virtues are inherent in the salvation experience, the focus here is on the consistent practice of these virtues in the context of every day life.

It is interesting to note that in Ephesians 5:18, the command to be filled with the Spirit is in the passive tense, indicating that it is an experience that results from the believer yielding to the indwelling Holy Spirit. No effort is required on the part of the believer to be filled with the Spirit. In Ephesians 6:13 the command to put on the full armor of God is an arost imperative, which means that the believer must put forth effort to dress up in God's armor. I should also point out that in both the filling and the dressing, the responsibility of the believer is to obey God's command and do it.

In dressing for this spiritual struggle the first piece of armor that is handed to the Christian soldier is the belt of truth. Ephesians 6:14 says, ". . . having girded [fastened] your loins with truth . . ." The idea of truth here is not the truth of the gospel by which the believer was saved. No, in this context, truth refers to the principle of truth, which resulted from believing the gospel and being saved.

This belt of truth is to be fastened around the loins of the believer next to the skin, so that the Christian soldier is able to move about both offensively and defensively in this life and death struggle with Satan and his demons. The belt of truth is honesty, pure motives—no hypocrisy in the believer's life and ministry. It is truth that will not permit deception, and fraud. It is truth that will not allow gossip and deceit. It is the truth that enables the believer to think the best about others until they can no longer do so.

"Take the belt of truth," the text says. It is to be fastened around your loins, so that the schemes of the devil will not be able to catch hold of your life and throw you down by way of a flawed character in the area of truth. Truth is for most Christians a major challenge in terms of relationships. This is especially true in the lives of single men in their relationship with women.

"Truth" is used four times in the fourth chapter of this book. It is used in 4:15 in the context of Christian fellowship—"speaking the truth in love" Spiritual growth is rooted in the soil of truth. In 4:21 truth is used as that which defines the very essence of Jesus—"just as truth is in Jesus." The foundation of Christian doctrine is truth in Jesus. It is used in 4: 24 as that which characterizes the new self that the believer is to put on after having pulled off the old self and been renewed in the spirit of the mind. "Put on the new self which in the likeness of God has been created in righteousness and holiness of the truth" It is used in 4: 25 as the expression of the new self in the context of the believer's social life—"Laying aside falsehood speak truth every man with his neighbor."

It must be noted that the text sets forth truth as that which first and foremost reveals the presence of the new self. "Speak the truth, one with the other."

The reason given in 4:25 that obligates believers to speak truth to one another is that we are members of one another. Every single man and woman must learn to relate to each other in such a way that it is evident that they recognize their eternal bond one to the other.

The issue of speaking the truth to one another is not merely a matter of deciding to get the facts straight. The real issue in speaking the truth is one of integrity. The issue of integrity is not just about correct information; it is really about the will to be transparent with people.

I find in the Christian community a number of saints who always get the facts straight so that they cannot be accused of lying. However, it is what they choose not to tells you, that is the issue. You see being truthful means being totally open with people so that they know what you know and think about the situation.

Personal integrity is about being the same in attitude and behavior in private as well as in public. The security belt of the believer is truth in the inner man. In this struggle with the adversary, the devil, genuineness is absolutely necessary.

In chapter four the issue for the believer is speaking the truth as an expression of a new life in Christ. In chapter six the focus is on fastening truth about the loins as a means of standing against the schemes of the devil, while continually struggling with those schemes.

In John 8:44 Jesus told the best religious people of His day that they were of their father, the devil, and the works of their father, the devil they would do. Then Jesus said he (the devil) was a liar from the beginning. In fact he (the devil) is the father of lies, being that he was a liar and a murderer from the beginning.

The whole life of a child of God must be characterized by truth in every relationship and in all ministry. The belt of truth is the believer's heart based on a commitment to genuineness. The belt of truth is the difference between the single saint who is nothing more than a "wanna be" and an authentic saint.

Having fastened the belt of truth around the loins, the believer is next handed the breastplate of righteousness. I take it that the belt of truth is designed and worn about the body in such a way that it makes the Christian soldier functional and agile in his/her struggle with the powers of evil. The breastplate of righteousness is designed to cover the vital organs and thus protect them from the weapons of the evil one.

This breastplate is designed to cover both the front and the back of the soldier. I am reminded here of Prov. 4:23: "Watch over your heart, for out of it flows the issue of life." I am also reminded of the words of Jesus:

"Where your treasure is there will your heart be also." Mark 7 says that it is out of the heart that the mouth speaks. Jeremiah 17:9 says, "The heart is the most deceitful thing there is and desperately wicked. No one can really know how bad it is."

I take it that in living and serving the Lord, being involved as we are in a life and death struggle with the powers of evil in this evil day, we must dress up with the kind of armor that protects our heart.

In considering these verses, it is important to note that the heart is inherently inclined towards that which is evil. Thus to stand in this struggle with the devil, the heart must be shielded from the power and influence of the devil. In addition, we must note that the human heart is such that whoever and whatever controls the heart, controls the individual. Thus, the human heart must be protected from its susceptibility to exploitation by the powers of evil.

In this struggle with Satan and the powers of evil, it is not just a matter of being shielded from the assault of the enemy, the heart must be kept from exposing itself to the schemes of the devil. I am saying that the heart of the believer is not altogether loyal to the cause of Christ. Thus it must be protected from the schemes of the devil that will induce it to commit treason against the kingdom of heaven. I have found over the years that many single Christians, while extensively involved in Christian service, have come to a time in their lives where their hearts are not in what they are doing in the name of Jesus. Be careful single saint that your heart not commit treason against the kingdom of heaven by exposing itself to the schemes of the enemy.

This piece of heart-protecting equipment is called "the breastplate of righteousness." The focus is on the content of this breastplate, namely, righteousness. The breastplate of righteousness is designed to protect the heart from the deceitful schemes of the devil—schemes to which even the saved heart is inherently inclined to accept. I am speaking here of that something inside of you and me that causes us to do evil even though we are trying to do good. (Rom. 7). You see, the flesh is prone to cooperate with the schemes of the devil.

This piece of equipment (the breastplate of righteousness) is not so much about protection from what others can do to you and me, as much as it is about what you and I are inclined to do that is harmful to our own testimony. In this evil day, pornography, lust, greed, deception, infidelity, etc., are all part and parcel of our culture. These are an integral part of what it means to be American. The devil knows full well that our heart is already disposed to enjoy any and all of these. Thus, while standing against the schemes of the devil, if we are not careful, we will lose our sensitivity to sin and lose the struggle with the adversary.

The breastplate of righteousness is a heart-level commitment to holiness in one's thinking, attitude and behavior. It's essential to our protection from the evil scheme of the devil who has the appearance of being harmlessly entertaining, but is in fact deadly. This is a character trait; it has to do with the kind of person one is in private as well as in public.

The breastplate of righteousness is the difference between being single who is secular in his/her thinking and behavior, and the kind of single who is God-focused. For the secular minded believer, church is nothing more than a social activity; there is no spiritual agenda.

The third piece of equipment is the gospel of peace. It is equipment fitted for the feet. In the Roman army, the soldiers had their feet shod with boots that were suited for their task. They had long cleats in them, fitted the feet well, were durable enough for travel over long distances and over rough ground. Even though the terrain was uneven, these sure footed soldiers were able to maneuver well and reach their destination.

For the believer the gospel of peace is about two things. First, it is about the gospel that saves the soul. It is that message that is based on and rooted in the death, burial and resurrection of Jesus Christ. It is about simple faith in that message alone for salvation. Second, the gospel of peace is about the effect of that gospel message on the heart of the believer, namely, peace with God combined with the piece of God.

With these two things in mind I conclude that the believer who has his/her feet shod with the preparation of the gospel, is one who is sure of personal salvation and is confident of God's grace, mercy and protection. This is the kind of Christian who is on his/her way to heaven and knows that. At the same time there is confidence in God's care and provision for them in this life right now.

Such a believer is sure footed in varied and different circumstances of life, so that, no matter what the situation, he/she is standing on sure doctrinal footing and cannot easily be pushed off balance.

This is the kind of believer who is able to make peace and serve as an advocate of reconciliation and unity in the church. Satan in his schemes often convinces the believer that he/she is not really saved nor really any different from anyone else. The believer who has on the proper footwear is able to resist this.

Having the feet shod with the preparation of the gospel means being able to always give an answer to anyone who asks you the reason for the hope you have in Christ. It gives one the ability to defend his/her faith in the risen Christ and the written word.

In conclusion, our struggle is not with flesh and blood but with the powers of evil. It is the responsibility of each and every believer to dress up in God's armor so that we will be able to stand individually and collectively. This armor is first and foremost equipment for the character. It is the kind of equipment that makes one authentic. This is not a struggle for "wanna be's"; only those who are genuine in their faith and walk with God will qualify.

## DRESSING UP FOR THE STRUGGLE

I am told by those who are supposed to know that the United States military has in its arsenal of artillery a helicopter called the "Cobra." This one piece of equipment is said to possess velocity and fire power capable of completely destroying a professional football stadium (the size of Texas stadium in Dallas, Texas) within seven seconds. With this kind of weapon aimed in one's direction, it is inconceivable to even think of escaping its destructive powers much less shielding one's self from its fire power.

In the war with Iraq the United States used scud missiles that literally decimated whole communities of people along with everything they owned. To be a target of the awesome military technology and fire power of America is to, in fact, be dead.

As I think about the military of our day and how wars are fought and won, it is clear to me that the individual soldier is hardly significant as an individual against the fire power of the opposing country. The military strategists of today target whole communities and countries not individuals. In order to kill one person or retaliate against one country, a whole plane full of people may be destroyed by a terrorist's bomb.

The weapon of choice on the streets among gangs is the AK47 with a one-hundred-round clip. I am told that an AK47 fires about six bullets a second, this means that in less than twenty seconds. This gun will fire one hundred times, killing and wounding hundreds of people. Many of the driveby shootings and killings are done with AK47s.

It is my contention that the fire power of the devil and his arsenal of spiritual military might is much like that of the super powers of our day. The trouble is that the church is equipping God's soldiers with bows and arrows to fight against the contemporary spiritual military arsenal of the Devil.

Current weapons like the Cobra or the scud missile are not biblical examples of what our struggle with the devil is like. To understand the spiritual struggle every believer is involved in, we must look back in history, not American history, but the history of the Roman soldier of the first century. The Roman soldier of the first century wore a strong belt around his loins. This belt was designed and worn to enable the soldier to move with deliberate skill and agility. The soldier also had on a breastplate that covered his back and his chest. This piece of equipment protected the vital organs so that he could survive the battle even if he received a frontal blow or an assault from the back. The soldier's boots had cleats that dug into the soil as they marched from one battle to the other. The cleated boots gave the solder solid footing as he negotiated terrain that was rough and rocky.

As we have looked at this dress of the Roman soldier, we have made the point that the armor that the Christian soldier puts on is all God's armor and the first three pieces of equipment are all about Christian character. The belt of truth is the believer's heart-based commitment to authenticity. It is the difference between the church member who is nothing more than a "wanna be" and a genuine saint. The breastplate of righteousness is a heart-level commitment to holiness in one's thinking, attitude and behavior. This is crucial for protection from the evil schemes of the devil. These demonic schemes most often have the appearance of being harmless and even entertaining. This is reflected in one's character. It has to do with the kind of man or woman we are in private and in public. For the believer, the gospel of peace encompasses two things: The gospel message and its effect. First, is the soul saving message that is based on and rooted in the death, burial and resurrection of Jesus Christ. It is about simple faith in that message alone for salvation. Second, the gospel of peace is about the result of that gospel message on the heart of the believer which is peace with God combined with the peace of God.

With the character equipment properly fitted, the Christian soldier is next handed the "shield of faith." "Take up the shield of faith with which you will be able to extinguish all the flaming missiles of the devil," exhorts Ephesians 6:16.

The shield that the Roman soldier carried was two feet wide and four feet long. It was made of wood and covered with rawhide. Before going out to battle the soldier would soak his shield in water so that when ignited arrows were launched by the enemy, the shield would not catch fire and burn, even though the flaming arrow penetrated the shield.

The soldier used the shield to protect himself from the arrows of the enemy both the burning and not burning. If for whatever reason the soldier let his shield down and was struck, that soldier immediately had three problems. First, he had an arrow in his body and was bleeding; second, his body was on fire; third, his shield was lowered and he was likely to be hit by additional arrows.

When a soldier was struck and lowered his shield due to the pain from the hit, the soldier next to him was exposed. In battle each soldier's shield was partial protection for the adjacent soldier. Thus when one soldier fell the one next to him most often was also knocked off by the enemy.

Ephesians 6:16 says, "In addition to all, [taking up] the shield of faith with which you will be able to extinguish all the flaming missiles of the evil one." This piece of equipment has dual functions. Not only does it have the defensive ability to block flaming missles, it also has the capability to extinguish all the flaming missiles of the evil one.

The flaming or burning arrows represent temptation to evil, impure thoughts, unloving behavior, false teaching, persecution, doubt, discouragement, despair, plus much, much more. All of these flaming arrows are in the hand of the devil and his demons and they are systematically fired at the child of God. The shield of faith in the hand of the believer is to be used to extinguish all such arrows.

It is important at this juncture to look at the word "faith." In Ephesians Paul used the word eight times.

1:15: "That is why, ever since I heard of your strong faith in the Lord Jesus and of the love you have for Christians everywhere" (*Living Bible*). Paul says to the saints at

Ephesians that it was the news of their faith in the crucified and risen Christ that caused him to pray for them. It was not news of their church membership or religious involvement that excited Paul; it was their faith in Jesus Christ.

2:8: "For by grace you have been saved through faith; and that not of yourselves, it is the gift of God" (*New American Standard Bible*). It the grace of God through faith that saves from sin. In other words, faith is the means by which a person is saved.

3:12: "In whom we have boldness and confident access through faith in Him" (*New American Standard Bible*). In the Christian life the resources from which the believer gets his/her boldness and confidence by which they access the presence of God is by means of their faith in the risen Lord Jesus.

3:17: "So that Christ may dwell in your hearts through faith; and that you, being rooted and grounded in love" (*New American Standard Bible*). It is the believers heart based faith in the risen Lord Jesus that roots and grounds him/her in the faith.

4:5: "One Lord, one faith, one baptism"(*New American Standard Bible*). Faith is the unifying factor in all of Christianity.

4:13: "Until we all attain to the unity of the faith, and of the knowledge of the Son of God, to a mature man, to the measure of the stature which belongs to the fullness of Christ" (*New American Standard Bible*). The goal of discipleship and Christian education is spiritual maturity in which there is unity of the faith.

6:23: "Peace be to the brethren, and love with faith, from God the Father and the Lord Jesus Christ" (*New American Standard Bible*). Faith and love are the heart and soul of the Christian doctrine.

6:16: "In addition to all, taking up the shield of faith with which you will be able to extinguish all the flaming missiles of the evil one" (*New American Standard Bible*). The same faith that caused Paul to Pray for the saints at Ephesians . . . the same faith that saved those to whom Paul wrote at Ephesians . . . the same faith that equipped the saints to live and walk with God and grow in their spiritual life is said to be the shield that extinguishes all the flaming arrows of the devil.

It is important to know that without faith it is impossible to please God. Without faith it is not possible to stand against the arrows of the devil. The question then must be—just what is this shield of faith that is so functional in our struggle with the devil? This shield of faith is the ability of the believer to draw upon all the resources that God has provided for him/her to be used at will in this struggle with the spiritual forces of wickedness in the heavenly places.

I have said that in preparation for war, the Roman soldier soaked his shield in water so that when it caught a flaming arrow from the enemy, the shield did not catch fire. The wet wood and the saturated animal skin extinguished the fire of the burning arrow. Christian soldiers must do likewise in preparation for their struggle with the devil. They must soak their shield of faith in the blood of Jesus so that when their faith is struck with the burning arrows of hard times, discouragement and persecution, their faith will not go up in flames but will instead extinguish the flames.

The enemy dipped his arrow in oil, set it ablaze and shot it at the target for the express purpose of intimidating and frightening the opposition. Often when the soldiers at whom the burning arrows were fired saw these incoming flaming missiles they would throw down their shields and run for cover. So it is with Christian soldiers in their struggle with the devil. The arrows that are fired at us by our adversary are designed to scare us so badly that we drop our shield of faith and run for the cover of doubt, depression and human reasoning.

I have seen many Christian women intimidated by the devil in regard to their single state. They have literally thrown down their faith and sought security in some shallow relationship with a pagan man. Others are scared into thinking that their biological clock is winding down so they had better grab whomever, get married and have children. Many are verbally told that their adulthood and womanhood are not validated until they have a ring on their finger . . . to wit—a man! Then there are those single men and women who are pushed to frustration and despair with God because they have not yet succeeded in other personal and professional pursuits. In all of these and many other situations the shield of faith is the only protection the Christian has.

What then is the stuff of which our shield of faith is made? The Christian's shield of faith is made up of the undeniable historical fact that God so loved the world that He gave His only begotten Son that whosoever believe in Him should not perish but shall have everlasting life.

The shield of faith is made up of the truth that Jesus, God's only son died on the cross on Calvary's mountain, was buried and rose three days later. This shield of faith is covered with the blood of Jesus and the justifying power of the resurrection.

Every single saint must know that since God has done all of this for him/her and since He did it all before He was loved by them, surely God will not withhold from them any good thing. The same faith by which this saint was saved must protect this saint from despair during difficult life circumstances. Faith is not only trusting God for what cannot be seen; it is in fact trusting God when there is nothing there to be seen. You see our God is a great big God and He can do anything He wants whenever He wants.

On resurrection morning the disciples of Jesus saw Him and bore witness to the fact that He Jesus was alive from the dead. Thomas, one of the twelve disciples somehow was absent when Jesus appeared to the other disciples. When he showed up, the disciples who had seen the resurrected Christ told Thomas that Jesus was alive from the dead. Thomas listened to what they said about Jesus being alive from the dead and then replied, "I do not believe this, and further I will not believe this thing you are saying to me unless and until I see it for myself and put my very own hands into the hole in Jesus' side, the hole I saw the Roman soldier put there. I must also see the nail prints in His hands. Now if I see all of that then and only then will I be persuaded that Jesus is alive from the dead."

It happened that by the time Thomas finished laying out the condition by which he could be persuaded, Jesus showed up. said to Thomas, "I heard what you said, take your hand and put it into my side and look here are the nail prints in my hand." When Thomas saw what he needed to see, he said, "Lord I believe."

Thomas in this experience was getting together his shield of faith. Thomas wanted to be able to say: "I am a witness of the fact that Jesus is alive from the dead." Thomas needed to be able to say something more than: "I heard the other disciples say they saw Him." Thomas needed to be able to say, "I saw Him for myself."

The single saint needs to be able to say for him/herself, "I know for myself that Jesus is alive from the dead . . . I know for myself that Jesus lives because He lives in my heart . . . I know for myself that Jesus is alive because He hears and answers my prayers." On Christ the solid rock you must stand; all other ground is sinking sand.

## GETTING YOUR HEAD STRAIGHT

When one looks at the helmet of the modern day football player and compares it with the helmet of football players of years past, it is evident that the game of football as it is played today is perceived to be far more physical, hard hitting and even dangerous, than it was in years past. The modern day football helmet is designed to protect the athletes head and neck from injury given the rough and tough nature of the game.

This new professional football helmet of today is reflective of two things: the kind of injuries sustained in the past and the value of the players. Much has been learned from playing the game of football over the years and the design of today's football helmet reflects this. It's constructed to minimize head and neck injuries unlike those of years past. The new helmet is also a reflection of the high value that the owners place on football players. These athletes have the ability to win games and winning is everything.

In the current United States military the helmet is used more for identification than for protection against the weapons of the enemy. It is virtually impossible for any helmet to protect against the modern day firepower of most opposing armies. Yet each country's military has its own unique helmet, designed to identify the soldier as belonging to this or that country.

It seems to me that in terms of successfully living the single life today many single men and women are wearing the helmet of years past. It is important that singles take into consideration the experiences of those singles of years past with a view to learning from those experiences. This knowledge can help determine what changes must be made in their head gear. Given the rough and tough nature of the spiritual struggle with the forces of evil that single saints face today, some alteration is necessary.

The local church must reevaluate its ministry to the singe families in the congregation, with a view to determining how best to maximize their effectiveness to this growing community of believers. To this end the church leaders must put greater emphasis on the single life as a valid (not pathetic) option for believers. Like the single saint, the local church leaders must match the head gear for them based on the with the nature of the struggle with the devil and his demons.

In the Roman army of years past, the soldier was issued each piece of the armor that he was to put on in preparation for battle. That is, each piece, with the exception of the helmet, was handed to him. When it came to the helmet, the soldier most often reached down and picked up his own helmet and placed it on his head. It is important to note that he took up his helmet before he took up his sword. Had he taken the sword before the helmet, he would not be able to take up his helmet. No soldier went forth to war without his helmet. The single person who determines to finish well in their life and service to their Lord must have on the proper head dress.

The helmet served as both protection and identification for the Roman soldier. It protected the soldier from the arrows of the enemy and it identified the solder as belonging to the Roman army.

Ephesians 6:17 says, "take up the helmet of salvation." This helmet of salvation, I take it is a reference to the believer identification with the army of the Lord Jesus. It protects the believer's head from the fiery missiles/arrows of the enemy. The helmet of salvation consists of the believer's present deliverance from the power, penalty and ultimately the very presence of sin.

In this spiritual struggle with the devil and his demons the believer stands in the present experience of being free from the dominating power, influence and control of sin over his/her life. In addition the believer has settled in his/her mind the reality of the hope of ultimate deliverance from the presence of sin.

So many single saints are trying to stand for Jesus in their life and service while at the same time struggling with the issue of whether or not they are genuinely saved. Having on the proper head gear in this struggle with the forces of evil means being clear in your head that you are genuinely saved. Salvation in this context has to do with victory over personal human depravity. It has to do with having one's head straight and assured as to whom one is and to whom one belongs.

It is important to say that without the helmet of salvation the believer is in danger of losing the struggle. This is due to uncertainty about who Jesus is and doctrinal intimidation as to what salvation really means.

Christians who do not don their helmet of salvation may be saved but they lack assurance of their salvation. They may have been born again but they do not have confidence in the eternality of their salvation.

Having on the helmet of salvation means that when it comes to an inquiry about who Jesus is and what salvation means, the believer is able to give an answer to any and everyone who asks for a reason of the hope that they have in Him. This hope in Jesus is not based on the saint's spiritual perfection but on a personal relationship with God through Jesus Christ.

The helmet of salvation is not so much about external circumstances affecting the believer as it is about what is settled internally in the mind and spirit of the believer while in the midst of these circumstances.

Much of the struggle with which the single saint must contend in standing against the schemes of the devil is related to the mind and spirit. The struggle is about steadfastness in the faith, mind and heart. It is about understanding what it is that all believers have in Christ Jesus. The helmet of salvation means knowing that every saint has an inheritance in Christ Jesus that cannot be altered by circumstances in this life.

This inheritance to which we have been appointed is said to be "In Him," [Eph. 1:4]. "In Him" refers to the risen Christ. However, we must pay close attention to the fact that there are prerequisites to obtaining this inheritance in Christ. As recorded in Ephesians 1:13 it occurs, "after listening to the message of truth, the gospel of your salvation." The text is saying that in order to gain access to this inheritance it is necessary to first hear the gospel message. The helmet of salvation is being cognizant of what it is we have as believers in Christ.

The single saint who does not have on the helmet of salvation will tend to focus on what it is they do not have in this life, with little focus on life eternal. The helmet of salvation equip the single saint to keep a clear head spiritually so that the focus is on his/her relationship with God through Jesus Christ no matter the circumstances in this life.

To have the helmet of salvation is to have clarity on the "how" of salvation. It is to be fully persuaded that salvation is free to all who would have it. The Bible says, "By grace we have been saved." Salvation by grace means that salvation is a gift from God. It is not possible to contribute anything to our salvation. Thus to say, "I joined the church," or "I grew up in church; therefore, I am saved," is to say that you are not saved. Salvation is a gift from God. By grace you are saved.

It is important to understand that being morally good will not obtain for you a right relationship with God. It is equally important to know that being morally bad will not sentence you to hell. It is true that saved folk will live righteously, but not all who so live are saved. It is also true that immoral people tend not to be saved; nevertheless, it is what people believe about Jesus that determines their eternal destiny, not the bad or good that they do. Salvation is a gift from God.

The helmet of salvation means having confidence in the eternality of salvation. It is to know beyond a shadow of a doubt that it is not possible to lose your salvation. Single saints must not think that every time they fail in their walk with God they need to be saved again.

It is interesting to note that Ephesians 4:30 focuses on the believer grieving the Holy Spirit "And do not grieve the Holy Spirit of God by whom you were sealed for the day of redemption." I think we must pay close attention to these words. Indeed it does teach that believers have been sealed by the Holy spirit for the day of redemption. It is not possible for anything or anybody to break that seal and take away our salvation.

Having put on the helmet of salvation the soldier picks up his final piece of equipment which is the sword of the spirit. Ephesians 6:17: "Take the sword of the Spirit which is the word of God." The text could read, "take the sword that belongs to the Spirit which is the word of God." We must note first and foremost that this sword that the soldier has is the word of God, in addition to belonging to the Holy Spirit.

The Roman soldier used his sword both offensively and defensively in his battle with the enemy. Without his sword the soldier could not stand against the assault of the enemy, nor could he effectively assault the enemy. The use of the sword in a battle meant that the soldier was engaged up close and personal with the enemy. The soldier did not customarily throw his sword at the enemy. The very life of the soldier most often depended on his ability to hold on to and effectively use his sword both offensively and defensively.

With this image in mind, I take it that as single Christians engaged in this spiritual struggle with the devil, success in standing in the struggle and thus finishing well in this up close and personal struggle with the enemy is dependent upon being proficient in handling the word of God. This means being seriously involved in either being discipled or discipling others.

In Luke 4 we have an example of how our Savior used the word of God defensively in his struggle with the devil. I should mention here that Jesus was Himself a single man. When the devil came after Jesus with the schemes of pride, natural desire and compromise, Jesus used the sword of the Spirit (the Word of God) to block and cast down these assaults.

The sword of the Spirit is the word of God, according to the text. I take it that this means that the believer must be fully convinced that the Bible in its entirety is inspired by God. To put it another way the child of God must know for sure that the Bible was not written and compiled by clever men and women who were determined to express their own opinion and ideas. Rather holy men and women penned the words as they were carried along by the Holy Spirit. The Bible is inspired of God. This means that every word of the Bible came from the mind and heart of the living God. The central agent in communicating the word of God to men and women was the Holy Spirit, thus it is in fact the sword of the Spirit.

In this struggle with the devil single saints must use the word of God to attack the schemes of the devil.

On the other hand, they must also use the word of God to defend themselves against the schemes of the devil.

The sword of the Spirit which is the word of God is the believer's weapon to be used is this spiritual struggle. Second Corinthians 10:4-5: "The weapon of our warfare are not carnal [but spiritual]."

## CONCLUSION

In the context of our day it is evident that sports are the "in" thing for most folk. It does not really matter whether the players are professional or just amateurs playing for the joy of it. It can almost be said that the athlete of today is revered almost as a god of some kind.

There is a prevailing attitude among a vast majority of folk today that winning at whatever the cost is the goal of any sports activity. In the name of winning almost anything and everything is sacrificed. The professional athlete can be as nasty as he/she wants to be . . . just keep on winning.

Though I know very little about most sports in terms of how the game is actually played, I have learned that no matter how good the athlete is, there is a coach who calls the shots. The player whether an offensive or defensive player, a rookie or an old pro is in constant communication with the coach, who is in touch with the head coach. It is not possible to play the game of football and win if the players are not in touch with the head coach.

The same is true of the soldier. No matter how well-equipped the soldier, unless he/she is in touch with the commander-in-chief, the whole battle can be lost. In any struggle with an enemy, it is not only necessary to understand the nature of the struggle and the enemy, it is also necessary to know who is in charge of the army and to be in constant touch with that person.

It has been my experience to observe that more than a few single saints try and live the Christian life in a social and spiritual vacuum—out of touch with reality. Many strive to be holy while being out of touch with the church and the body of believers. Still others think that spouting the right spiritual jargon means that they are in touch with God.

The Christian soldier at this point is fully aware of the nature of the struggle. He knows that the enemy is not flesh and blood but all the powers of evil. The soldier is clear on his/her assignment, namely, to stand against the forces of evil in this evil day. The soldier is fully dressed in all of God's spiritual armor: (1) the belt of truth, (2) the breastplate of righteousness, (3) the boots of the gospel of peace, (4) the shield of faith, (5) the helmet of salvation, and (6) the sword of the Spirit which is the word of God.

We must not think that the soldier is fully prepared for the struggle because he/she has on all of the right equipment. Being properly dressed in the armor of God is a prerequisite to engaging in the struggle with the devil and his demons. All of the armor that the soldier has on belongs to God. In addition, everything the solder of the Lord has on has made him/her dependent on the Lord. Single Christians must resist the idea that independence is the way to go. The single saint who attempts to stand alone in a struggle with the devil and his demons will not stand. The whole of the armor of God is designed to make the believer dependent upon Him . . . creating the absolute necessity of being in constant touch with Him in prayer.

Ephesians 6:18 says, "with all prayer and petition pray at all times in the Spirit." I take it that the text is saying that to finish well in our struggle with the powers of evil, the believer must be in constant touch with the living Lord Jesus Christ. The question that must be asked at this point is: "Are you in touch with Jesus?" I am not asking if you are saved or not, nor am I asking if you know who the enemy is; I am not even asking if you are properly dressed for the struggle. My question is, are you in touch with Jesus? In other words are you constantly talking to the one in whose victory over all the forces of evil you are standing?

Ephesians 6:18 continues, "and with this in view be

on the alert with all perseverance and petition for all the saints." When the text says "with this in view" it is referring to the statement "with all prayer and petition pray at all times in the Spirit." Thus the child of God who is to finish well in the spiritual struggle is characterized as one who has an attitude of prayer and a spirit of alertness.

As it pertains to prayer more than a few Christian, single and married, are not at all alert. The call from the Lord to the Christian soldier to be alert is reflective of the fact that we are in evil days and seriously engaged in a spiritual struggle with the powers of evil.

Ephesians 5:16 says that we must make the most of every minute we have because the days are evil. I take it that the call of God today is for all of us (His children) to be on the alert and about the business of standing and shining as His light in this evil day. Sometimes it is necessary for some of God's children to cast their light into an area of darkness that others are not fitted for. Each of us must know for ourselves what it is that God has called us to, so that we do not spend our time unwisely. The saint who knows what it is that God has called him/her to do and is in touch with the living God in prayer is able to distinguish between that which seems to be important but is not and that which seems to be important, and really is.

Ephesians 6:18 says, "pray at all times in the Spirit" The text is saying that being in touch with the living God means praying in the power of the Holy Spirit. Consider the role of the Holy Spirit in the life of the child of God as presented in Ephesians:

(1) 1:13—In Him, you also, after listening to the message of truth, the gospel of your salvation—having also believed, you were sealed in Him with the Holy Spirit of promise,

(2) 2:18—for through Him we both have our access in one Spirit to the Father;

(3) 3:16—that He would grant you, according to the riches of His glory, to be strengthened with power through His Spirit in the inner man;

(4)   5:18—And do not get drunk with wine, for that is dissipation, but be filled with the Spirit;

(5)   5:17—And take the helmet of salvation, and the sword of the Spirit, which is the word of God;

(6)   5:18—With all prayer and petition pray at all times in the Spirit, and with this in view, be on the alert with all perseverance and petition for all the saints.

Being in touch with the living God means knowing the role of the Holy Spirit in the life and service of the believer. These verses from Ephesians tells us six things about the role of the Holy spirit in our lives:

- We are sealed in Him (Christ) with the Holy Spirit of promise;
- We have access in one Spirit (the Holy Spirit) to the Father;
- We are strengthened with power through His Spirit (the Holy Spirit);
- We are to be filled with the (Holy) Spirit;
- We have the sword of the (Holy) Spirit, which is the word of God;
- We are to pray at all times in the (Holy) Spirit.

I find it both interesting and instructive that the text says to pray in the Spirit. You see praying in the Spirit to the living God means talking to God the Father in the Name of the Son but through the medium of the Holy Spirit. It is helpful to know that the same Holy Spirit of God that is so involved in our walk with God is the agent through whom we keep in touch with the Father. Praying is a supernatural thing that requires the enabling power of God the Holy Spirit.

We must pay attention to the words prayer, perseverance, and alertness. These words suggest that in this spiritual battle with the devil and his demons, the believer's ability to persevere and remain constantly alert is dependent upon that believer's prayer life. It is possible to have on all of the right spiritual gear and not be able to stand your ground in this struggle with evil forces. **The key to standing is prayer.**

# NOTES

# NOTES

# NOTES

# NOTES

# NOTES

# NOTES